I Wish I'd Known This

6 Career-Accelerating Secrets for Women Leaders

BRENDA WENSIL AND KATHRYN HEATH

BK

Berrett–Koehler Publishers, Inc.

Berrett-Koehler Publishers, Inc.
1333 Broadway, Suite 1000
Oakland, CA 94612-1921
Tel: (510) 817-2277
Fax: (510) 817-2278
www.bkconnection.com

ORDERING INFORMATION

Quantity sales. Special discounts are available on quantity purchases by corporations, associations, and others. For details, contact the "Special Sales Department" at the Berrett-Koehler address above.

Individual sales. Berrett-Koehler publications are available through most bookstores. They can also be ordered directly from Berrett-Koehler: Tel: (800) 929-2929; Fax: (802) 864-7626; www.bkconnection.com.

Orders for college textbook / course adoption use. Please contact Berrett-Koehler: Tel: (800) 929-2929; Fax: (802) 864-7626.

Distributed to the U.S. trade and internationally by Penguin Random House Publisher Services.

Berrett-Koehler and the BK logo are registered trademarks of Berrett-Koehler Publishers, Inc.

Printed in the United States of America

Berrett-Koehler books are printed on long-lasting acid-free paper. When it is available, we choose paper that has been manufactured by environmentally responsible processes. These may include using trees grown in sustainable forests, incorporating recycled paper, minimizing chlorine in bleaching, or recycling the energy produced at the paper mill.

Library of Congress Cataloging-in-Publication Data

Names: Wensil, Brenda, author. | Heath, Kathryn, author.
Title: I wish I'd known this : 6 career-accelerating secrets for women leaders / Brenda Wensil, Kathryn Heath.
Description: First edition. | Oakland, CA : Berrett-Koehler Publishers, [2022] | Includes bibliographical references and index.
Identifiers: LCCN 2021062831 (print) | LCCN 2021062832 (ebook) | ISBN 9781523000975 (paperback ; alk. paper) | ISBN 9781523000982 (pdf) | ISBN 9781523000999 (epub)
Subjects: LCSH: Women executives. | Women professional employees. | Career development. | Women—Vocational guidance.
Classification: LCC HD6054.3 .W45 2022 (print) | LCC HD6054.3 (ebook) | DDC 650.1082—dc23/eng/20220401
LC record available at https://lccn.loc.gov/2021062831
LC ebook record available at https://lccn.loc.gov/2021062832

First Edition
30 29 28 27 26 25 24 23 22   10 9 8 7 6 5 4 3 2 1

Book production: Seventeenth Street Studios
Cover design: Adrian Morgan

*To the generations of amazing women leaders
who have, and will, change our world for the better.*

CONTENTS

Broom on Fire

We wish this could be a conversation.

Ideally, you'd see our faces and we'd see yours. We would love to chat in person about the challenges women encounter while managing a career. We'd love to hear your problems and stories and ideas for the future and to share all we've learned. We would love to have that conversation with you.

This book is intended to be the next best thing: two master executive coaches sitting in your passenger seat, guiding you through a few of the typical obstacles of professional life. Our desire is to illuminate the most dangerous career blind spots you face in the workplace, help you sharpen your vision, and show you how to avoid common obstacles so many women encounter. We want to help you reach your finish line—the leadership position you want and a successful, sustainable career.

We know you have many options when it comes to career advice, and to be honest, we weren't looking for another book to write. However, our passion for helping women become successful, effective leaders has never been stronger. The need for women leaders has never been more urgent. And it's not just us saying that.

In 2021, in the midst of the global COVID pandemic, McKinsey & Company, in partnership with LeanIn.org, released its seventh annual *Women in the Workforce* report, based on surveys and interviews with 65,000 people who work in 423 companies.[1] This annual report continues to show that women have difficulty moving up the pipeline into higher levels.

We would like to see the infamous glass ceiling disappear altogether. One of the issues that must be addressed in order to make that happen is fixing a phenomenon that the report calls "the broken rung."[2] This term refers to the fact that women are disproportionately blocked at the first step toward a career in management. In 2021, for every 100 men who were promoted to managerial positions, only 86 women were promoted. McKinsey & Company note that "this makes it nearly impossible for companies to lay a foundation for sustained progress at more senior levels."[3] This gap is significantly wider for women of color, who account for only 4 percent of C-suite leaders.[4] Although women left the workforce in much higher numbers than men during the pandemic, the management gap cannot be attributed to attrition alone.

In *Break Your Own Rules*, Kathryn and her coauthors Mary Davis Holt and Jill Flynn cited research showing that companies' profits and share performance improve when women are well represented in senior leadership.[5] After studying 215 Fortune 500 companies for nineteen years, marketing professor Roy Adler found that firms with a higher number of female executives outperformed their competitors financially.[6] Business professors Cristian L. Dezső and David Gaddis Ross, who tracked

1,500 U.S. companies from 1992 to 2006, found a direct, positive correlation between the number of senior women managers and financial performance, market value, and sales growth.[7]

Those findings are holding steady in many other research studies. Among them is a 2020 McKinsey report using data that encompassed more than 1,000 large companies in fifteen countries. It found that "the greater the representation [of women], the higher the likelihood of outperformance. Companies with more than 30 percent women executives were more likely to outperform companies where this percentage ranged from 10 to 30, and in turn, these companies were more likely to outperform those with even fewer women executives, or none at all."[8]

A 2019 McKinsey study showed that women more frequently apply the leadership traits that are highly applicable to our complex global challenges, including inspiration, participatory decision-making, people development, and role modeling.[9]

The research is abundant. Clearly, we can't afford to lose women leaders. More important, it's clear that businesses urgently need more women who are ready and able to fill leadership positions. This serves as an additional impetus for writing this book.

THE BURNING BROOM

Our endeavor with this book is the professional equivalent of the heroic actions of a woman named Peggy whose resourcefulness and bravery helped avert a tragedy during World War II. Peggy was among the women all over the nation who supported the war effort by filling jobs in the community where many employers needed workers after men joined the military. Among these women was a small group in a U.S. town who served their country at a regional airport by standing watch in a tower to assist airplane pilots as they took off and landed.

From their perch in the tower, the women had a clear view of the airfield, the landscape along the horizon, and the railroad lines that ran near the airport. Their duties were mostly routine; they were responsible for sending clearance signals and radio messages to crews on the ground.

Peggy was a member of that tower. She and her co-workers could see the landing strip and watch planes ascend and grow smaller until they could no longer be seen from the tower. The women memorized railway schedules and looked out and down to watch trains pull in and out of the nearby rail yards.

One cold night, Peggy was on duty alongside two colleagues. Their routine was shattered when they spotted the flickering lights of a small aircraft making its way toward the landing area. The plane quickly dropped altitude before crashing onto the railroad tracks next to the airfield. Debris from the wreck stretched for a quarter of a mile along the train tracks. Following protocol, Peggy and her team sent out emergency requests for help.

Just a few minutes later, the women in the tower spotted a long train in the distance, unknowingly on a collision course with the demolished plane and its debris. From their vantage point, they could see another disaster about to unfold. Because of a bend in the tracks, the train's conductor would be unable to see the wreckage until it was too late to stop.

While her colleagues worked the radios in a desperate attempt to get help, Peggy felt compelled to act. She had to do something. She sprinted down the tower stairwell. On the first floor, she grabbed a heavy broom and a box of matches before racing out into the cold air. Running to the edge of the railroad track somewhere between the aircraft debris and the oncoming train, she lit the broom on fire and stepped onto the track. Holding the broom overhead, she ran toward the oncoming train. After rounding the curve, Peggy stopped briefly to relight the broom and began waving it again as she ran toward the white headlights, which were growing ever larger. Finally, completely spent, she stood in the middle of the track, frantically waving the flaming broom, desperately hoping the conductor could see her.

When the conductor caught sight of the small flicker of the broom's flame waving back and forth, the crew slowed the train before it rounded the bend. It screeched to a full stop just before it reached the mangled aircraft that littered the tracks. Without a doubt, one woman's determination prevented a seemingly inevitable disaster.

Peggy's dramatic broom-on-fire story is a metaphor for the work we do and what we want to accomplish with this book. In these chapters, we are lighting a symbolic broom on fire and running toward multiple generations of women in the workforce, warning them of imminent career blind spots around the bend. We know these blind spots. We've experienced them firsthand—and we have the scars to prove it. We also have deep understanding of blind spots from our coaching experience.

As master coaches, we have listened to and worked with female executives, middle managers, and supervising professionals across diverse industries, geographies, and cultures who come from every generation in the workforce. We've worked in multinational companies, midsize businesses, and nonprofit organizations, mostly with women whose companies have identified them as high-potential employees. A big part of the leadership coaching we do involves conducting 360-degree feedback assessments about the women we are working with. This entails interviewing ten or more people, on average, about what our client is good at and what could make her more effective. Our goal is to discover what she needs to learn and do to get to the next leadership level. After we have gathered that information, we prepare an extensive report and review it with the woman we are coaching. We've done thousands of these, and they never fail to turn up perceptions or patterns of behavior the clients were unaware of. The feedback brings these perceptions into the light and empowers the women we coach to deal with them.

The findings outlined in this book are based on twenty years of research, two books, countless articles and blog posts, and decades of coaching as well as our own long corporate careers (see figure 1). What we've discovered are a half-dozen ubiquitous blind spots that can keep women from accelerating into key leadership positions and attaining successful, sustainable careers.

As we coach women about their blind spots and the strategies for working with them, they often tell us, "I wish I'd known this earlier." With this book, you'll have the benefit of this information right now as you are charting the various phases of your career.

Our work with corporations is another layer of experience we bring. We know that cultures and norms aren't always accommodating and welcoming to today's diverse workforce, and part of our work with companies is to help them see this and make changes. We also do a lot of work around culture, those informal

WHERE WE GOT OUR DATA

The two of us have coached more than 800 women.

We have done more than 4,000 interviews for 360-degree reports.

Our firm has done three major research projects to discover how to help women in corporate America be more successful.

Figure 1. The sources of our data

unspoken rules and norms that exist in every company. We've found that these norms get communicated to men more frequently than to women. Our goal here is to illuminate these unwritten, informal secrets that for many complex reasons frequently don't filter to women.

When the women we work with are together, we often hear conversations about the double binds women leaders face in the workplace. Women have a sense that the rules are different for them, that when they act in the ways they see men acting in the workplace, they don't get the same reactions or results. Relief is evident as these women talk. They realize that they're not alone in their experiences. They start to see how expectations differ. They begin to see more clearly the cultural and societal messages constantly delivered to them about how they're supposed to behave in the world and realize that these messages are quite different from those that men receive. They begin to have a sense that some of the challenges they face aren't happening because they're deficient or substandard or inferior—they're just operating in circumstances that are often out of their control. Expectations for women are often different. We recognize that this can create a sense of injustice and frustration.

However, our singular intention in this book is to help you forestall missed opportunities and disrupt unhelpful patterns. The successful women we have analyzed have all mastered the skills in this book and leveraged them to their advantage. This book is focused on what we have learned and what we know works. It's about teaching you, the reader, to be intentional and purposeful about how you manage your career.

THE GROUNDHOG DAY INSPIRATION

The realization that this book was needed came at the end of a particularly long week of coaching and facilitating groups of women leaders. As we recapped the week, we were struck by how often the same handful of themes emerged throughout our work, like little video snippets on a continuous loop, no matter how different our audiences or how diverse our clients. As we talked about it, Kathryn joked, "I'm hearing the same topics and issues in almost every conversation I have. Sometimes it feels like we're stuck in Groundhog Day."

She was referring, of course, to the 1993 film starring Bill Murray and Andie McDowell. Murray plays a sarcastic, somewhat clueless TV weather forecaster who is sent to cover the annual Groundhog Day celebration in Punxsutawney, Pennsylvania, and finds himself caught in a time loop. Each morning, Groundhog Day begins again until he finally breaks the cycle by learning from his mistakes and changing his approach to life.[10]

We don't use the Groundhog Day metaphor lightly, and the insight was based on decades of our work. This book distills our research findings to the most common and the most important challenges women face in the workplace as they construct careers. Blind spots left unattended are derailers. This work is designed to help you navigate around them and accelerate beyond them.

Everyone has blind spots. Our goal is to bring them out of the shadows, where they can be examined, considered, and avoided. We consider this information to be empowering—choices can be made with fresh knowledge about how women are often perceived by those they work with. Leveraging this valuable feedback, women can edit their behavior, better adapt to the culture they are in, and understand how they're unintentionally getting in their own way.

Research and our experience has shown that women will be better served if they plot a professional course and aim higher in their careers with intention and purpose. There are many of reasons for this, but in the end, what matters most is that established patterns can be disrupted. This book offers you a half-dozen key evidence-based insights and many strategies designed to help you get clear about where you want to go. It will show you how to construct an effective, efficient roadway to get there—even if you can't always see what lies ahead.

In *Outliers: The Story of Success*, Malcolm Gladwell writes about the concept of the "10,000-Hour Rule."[11] While there are many nuances around what to practice and how, Gladwell is suggesting that the right focus over an extended period of time increases the likelihood that a person will achieve proficiency in a given skill. We have been coaching for a long time in a very specific way and we have learnings to pass along. One of our foundational messages is the imperative of being intentional, deliberate, and exceptionally clear about the outcomes you seek. Be purposeful about your career. Own it.

OUR VISION

When Katharine Graham was named CEO of the *Washington Post* in 1972, the first glass ceiling in the Fortune 500 was shattered.[12] In the last few decades, more women have (finally) taken their places as CEOs of major corporations. In the period 1995 to 2013, 7.4 percent of CEOs of Fortune 500 companies were women. Between 2014 and 2021 that number crept up to 8.2 percent, or 41 women.[13]

More than a decade ago, the women in our company created a vision. We imagined a world where (at least) 30 percent of the top jobs in corporate America would be held by women. (At the time, the number was about 17 percent.)[14] We decided to anchor this dream in a goal, which we called our Red Suit Vision. We pictured an executive meeting where ten leaders sat around the table making important decisions for a company—seven of them men in traditional business gray and three women clad in power red, changing the conversation and putting an important stake in the ground for the future of the firm. It wasn't that we thought 30 percent would be enough women leaders—it was a benchmark where we believed the numbers would make a profound difference.

Part of our goal was to support and empower women, but we also know that more women in leadership improves workplaces in general. As mentioned earlier, research has shown that businesses owned and led by women significantly outperform other businesses, particularly in essential areas such as profitability, innovation, diversity, and risk management.[15] This data inspired us in our quest. It compelled us to do amazing work with Fortune 100 organizations across the globe and with the women who work in all levels of these organizations.

Over the years, we saw a movement taking hold inside the organizations we worked with. Women began to find their voices. They raised their hands for the next challenge, scoured the landscape for new opportunities, and used their voices to influence key decisions. They discovered their personal power by crafting a vision and breaking the old rules. The awareness and enthusiasm were contagious. Leadership teams realized their investment in female leaders and executives paid off and cascaded into additional benefits for their businesses. We estimate that for each female professional we reached, what they learned and how they changed benefited an additional three to five colleagues of all genders. We have found that women are extremely generous. When they learn as professionals, they pass their knowledge on.

Research in late 2020 showed that 24 percent of C-suite roles were held by women. This was an improvement from 2011, but it is not nearly good enough.[16] One unique challenge we didn't foresee was the pandemic that began in 2020 that set back far too many working women. We recognize that there were also more serious, negative impacts on women of color and other marginalized groups. In our work and in this book, our focus is on women, in all their diversity, all over the world.

We don't want to neglect to say, emphatically, that this necessary work cannot be solely the responsibility of women. We recognize that women are challenged by systemic dynamics that are outside of their control. Men, dominant groups, company cultures, and policies all must change in order to get us to our goal of more women leaders in the workplace.

No one size can fit all. Everyone has their own personal journey. But we also know, because we have seen it happen, that great careers can be forged when professional women focus on specific strategies and behaviors. By illuminating common blind spots, we intend to help women stay on a fast and efficient career track.

The truth is, even if we had achieved our goal, we were never going to stop at 30 percent of women in senior leadership. Our work—and yours—continues. By illuminating the road ahead, women can become the intentional owners of deliberate careers.

USING THIS BOOK

Our research and our work among the thousands of career women we've coached over the decades has helped us identify six common blind spots. This has been hidden information for a long time and women haven't had access to it. We are revealing these business secrets in this book. (And we'd love for you to share these secrets with as many women as you can!)

These six blind spots sometimes overlap, but they're also distinct. They are connected to you and the woman you want to be in the world, but they are also associated with how others perceive you. Women have a deep desire to be authentic—and that is what we want for them. However, we want you to understand that people's perceptions can make a difference to your career and that you can have a hand in shaping those perceptions without sacrificing authenticity.

Because we can't have that wished-for conversation with each reader, chapters have been designed to mimic what we do with our coaching clients, with slight shifts to accommodate the context of a book.

We will be giving you a lot of information. It might seem like we're asking you to eat an elephant in one meal, but that's not our intention. Instead, please find the "bites" that seem most relevant and potentially satisfying for your career development and start there. When you feel ready, you can move on to another course.

Chapter titles identify each blind spot and tell you what requires your attention on the way to a successful, sustainable career. Themes covered in the next six chapters include:

Creating a compelling vision, establishing a direction, and developing an action plan.

Developing profound self-awareness through reflection, soliciting feedback, and becoming more intentional.

Establishing clear "reputationality," our word for mindfully establishing, shepherding, and communicating your reputation and your personal brand.

Creating a robust guidance system and consistently cultivating feedback to keep you on your career course (or to help you alter it).

Preparing and practicing relentlessly, especially in areas that fall outside the rubric of getting the job done.

Establishing a solid support system, or "posse," that can augment, reinforce, and offer counsel about your career choices.

We include stories in the chapters so you can see that the women we work with are just like you—bright, competent, and hard working. These stories provide details about someone who experienced a setback because of a blind spot. They're based on real women we have worked with, although their names have been changed to protect privacy.

Each chapter has a section that defines the blind spot the story illustrates, with the understanding that it is one that has emerged with thousands of other women. We explain why recognizing the blind spot is important. This is our version of waving the burning broom so you can avoid potential unseen obstacles on the road to an effective, sustainable career.

This is followed by a section called Perils of the Blind Spot that provides additional details about why attending to the blind spot is so important. Nobody intends for their career to crash and burn, but you can't respond to potentially dangerous situations if you don't see them or understand what might be around the bend.

The next section, Coach on Your Shoulder, offers questions designed to help you reflect about your current career and stimulate your thinking about ways you might be living in the blind spot. These questions are designed to help you start considering what you might do differently to avoid dangers that can harm your career. The questions will challenge your frame of reference and help you see other possibilities. We encourage you to pause here for self-reflection. If you find using a journal or taking notes useful, we encourage you to spend a few minutes writing down some of the answers or insights the coaching questions might have sparked.

We encourage you to keep your answers in mind as you read the section titled Strategies, which includes time- and experience-tested methods based on the decades of work we've done with clients who've employed them to overcome challenges and construct successful careers. By integrating some of these strategies into your work practices, you can make real-time changes that will help you shift your perspective, develop new habits, and overcome stumbling blocks. The goal in all these strategies is to help you develop new thought patterns and skills, create additional opportunities for yourself, expand your influence, and boost your confidence.

These suggested approaches aim to get you where you want to be in a more efficient, less stressful way. They can be employed at any stage of a career, but if you're just starting out, adopting some of these suggestions could give you an exponential boost as you build a deliberate and fulfilling career. We will offer many strategies. Remember to take moderate bites and chew thoroughly. Our recommendation is that you start with one area. Work on one thing before moving to another. It's not possible to tackle everything at once, and you shouldn't try to do so. Start with what resonates and seems manageable for you and build from there. We find that change happens more successfully when you take the time to focus and master something new.

The next section, Stories That Hold Us Back, takes a look at the common stories women tell themselves, often unconsciously. Even though they might not be aware of these stories, we've discovered that most women consistently hear the same sorts of mental messages, many of them negative. These messages and stories are rarely true, but they have great potential for holding women back. They're based on what we call limiting beliefs, and we all have them. We want you to notice them, examine them, and question them. Some of these stories in your head might work for you, but many of them can impede your progress and career trajectory. We suggest ways to create new stories that will bolster your self-awareness and deliberate career efforts.

A section titled The Power of Reframing: A New Story begins with the stories of clients (just like you) we've worked with over the years. These are the tales of women who have altered their stories, developed strategies, learned skills, and changed their ways of working. This is followed by suggestions for revisiting, revising and reframing your stories. Replacing your limiting beliefs with better, more productive stories and messages can foster a change in habits and patterns. Psychologists call this cognitive reframing. It is about identifying and changing the way you view situations, experiences, events, and emotions.

The inspiration is followed up with another Coach on Your Shoulder section that includes our best tips and practical advice. The section is designed to stimulate reflection on what you're doing now and how that's working for you and perhaps prompt you to think about alternative actions that could spur your career journey in a more fruitful and satisfying direction.

We end each chapter about blind spots with a summary of the key points made throughout the chapter. They highlight what we want you to know and take action on.

Chapter 7 isn't about a blind spot, exactly. It provides an opportunity for you to reflect on the most pervasive theme of our time—balancing the demands of work and life. Finding ways to address this challenge that work for you and the people in your life is essential to sustaining your energy and your career.

We continue to be inspired by the dream of a much larger percentage of women holding top leadership positions in companies throughout the world. We hold on to the dream because we know that when more women are leaders, the goals and direction of businesses and companies will change for the better and everyone will share in the benefits.

We are rooting for you. We want you to succeed. We want you to have a fulfilling, sustainable, and accomplished career. We want you to help fill the need for female leadership in all levels of every company, corporation, and industry. We offer you solid, evidence-based ways to avoid the blind spots. We want you to know this information now.

Let's get started—we'll light the broom.

CHAPTER ONE

Career Drift

You Need a Vision, Strategies, and a Plan

Anything you can imagine, you can create.

—OPRAH WINFREY

Corinna, a midcareer manager at a large professional services company, found herself in a quandary. She had strong technical skills and an aptitude for leadership and had been tagged by senior leaders as someone with high potential. We'd been asked to work with her because of the theme that cropped up in Corinna's feedback assessment again and again.

People made comments such as, "She's competent, but I have no idea what she wants to do long-term," "I'd like to help her, but I don't have a clue where she wants to land," and "She's likable and a hard worker. But if she has career goals, I'm unaware of them."

As Brenda discussed the major motif that had emerged in the feedback, Corinna expressed surprise about her colleagues' perception that she had no vision for her career development. But when Brenda asked her if she had career goals, her answer was nebulous. "Kinda," she said. Corinna had a desire to head "north," but she couldn't define how far north and couldn't visualize how she might start moving north. She struggled to describe the destination she was aiming for. She told Brenda that she found some areas in the company more interesting than others. She knew she wanted to be promoted. Corinna had not really established concrete goals and a career plan to get her there.

What do you want to be when you grow up? When children are asked this question, they often excitedly discuss their "grown-up" visions of themselves—sometimes several possibilities at once. "A firefighter, an artist, an astronaut, and a teacher. And maybe a doctor." Their answers change from day to day and week to week. That works for kids. They're supposed to imagine and explore and they have years to figure it out. For adults, it's a little trickier. They need something more concrete.

Establishing a career plan can help you define your direction, build capacity and confidence, and forestall missed opportunities. Clarity about where you want to end up will help you disrupt unhelpful patterns that distract from your vision, and as your career develops, you'll be able to more quickly spot when you should amend your plan or create a new one.

In our experience, lack of a career vision applies to men and women more than most of the blind spots we will be writing about. We've found that many people aren't very clear about where they want to land in their careers.

However, we also know that messages about the importance of mapping out a career don't go out as early and as often to women as they do to male colleagues. Educational institutions don't typically promote career planning; the focus tends to be about deciding how you want to earn a living, earning the degree, and landing your first job. And once you're employed, most companies don't devote resources to helping employees craft a vision for their careers. Too often, the organizational chart becomes the default and progress is measured by whatever promotion opportunities are available and secured at any given time.

In addition, women are more likely to be stymied by double binds and gender stereotypes. One glaring example: how often are men asked whether they will be returning to work after a new baby is born or adopted? While we recognize and welcome changes that allow men to be more connected to family, such as parental leave and flexible work schedules, we'd love to see the assumptions made about women as they navigate their careers and their families disappear. It's still common for women to feel more crunched for time than men because women typically take on a greater portion of the emotional and organizational labor of running their families.

Many of the double binds for women are more subtle. A 2018 article in the *Harvard Business Review* points out that women are expected to exhibit warmth and kindness, but when they do so, they are seen as less competent or rigorous. Women are told they must be authoritative to be considered credible, but when they are, they're also seen as arrogant. They are expected to serve others and the business but are viewed with suspicion if they advocate service to themselves.[1]

For these reasons and others, it's particularly important for women to be intentional about creating a vision for their careers and establishing clear plans and goals about how to achieve it.

Researchers Dasie Schultz and Christine Enslin point to studies showing that intentional career planning helps women navigate obstacles to advancement and proactively overcome gender bias and stereotypes on their journey to attaining executive level leadership positions. "Career planning was identified as one of the unwritten rules to advancement for women in organizations, and female executives who participated in past research studies exploring the hurdles to advancement for women wished they had discovered and applied career planning earlier."[2]

On the rare occasions when we hear women talk about career plans, the blueprint is typically sketchy, and most of the women we work with who have goals haven't thought through the concrete steps they must take to achieve them. We see too many women who are reluctant to step into their ambition and own it.

This is a major blind spot, and we get consistent evidence of this in the 360-degree feedback assessments we do for women. This invaluable tool gives us data and information from a cross-section of people who know the women we're coaching: colleagues, team members, direct reports, bosses, and other business stakeholders. Among the questions we ask are: "What is she good at? How could she be more effective? What does she need to do to get to the next level?"

Our feedback reports contain a common theme: vague expressions about the direction the women want to go. When you get that kind of feedback from the people you work closely with, it's a wake-up call to make a change. If you don't make your preferred destination clear to yourself and others, your career path might well become happenstance rather than deliberate.

Imagine a conversation with the CEO of a business who didn't know where to take the company. What if the company's business plan was a vague notion of "earning money"? Would you invest in a company with a mission statement that consisted of "Let's see what happens next"?

If you're going to be in charge of your career, you have to think like a CEO. And that means getting clear about your direction, establishing goals, and developing a strategy for achieving them.

THE BLIND SPOT: CAREER DRIFTING

Women don't hesitate to work on strategy or use critical thinking skills to benefit their companies, their teams, and their projects, yet they often don't apply that same level of creativity and strategic thinking to their careers. Because women tend to be rooted in the moment and focused on doing well in their day-to-day work, they can become blind to the importance of establishing a career vision. They haven't thought much about why it's important, so they often neglect to do it. This can be a blind spot in the same way that navigating to a destination without knowing its location would be. If you don't know exactly where you want to go, how will you find a map or ask for directions? You're at risk for getting lost or stuck in a place you don't want to be.

Without a focused career plan, women are more likely to follow a mentor, an advocate, or a sponsor into whatever role or opportunity is presented to them. Many women go with the flow of what the company needs instead of designing a career and intentionally charting their course. We see this all the time. It isn't wrong, exactly. It's just that "going with the flow" has a real chance of taking you to a place where you're not that excited to be. If you allow other people to manage your career—even unconsciously—there is a risk that they'll steer you to the places that serve them or the organization without accounting for your desires and strengths. You could end up sidelined or in a role that doesn't leave you fulfilled. You'll end up with a default career. Not having a plan can delay your ascent, create anxiety, and leave you with a sense of having no control over a major segment of your life. "There are no 'job fairies' who magically make a dream job appear," says Lynne Ford, CEO of MissionSquare Retirement. "You have to go out and get what you want."[3]

The most effective CEOs, those who are most likely to make an impact, have a plan. They know where they want to go, they deliberately scan the horizon for growth opportunities, and they overcome challenges and obstacles. CEOs study the environment to find that competitive advantage. You can do that too, if you're aware of where you want to land and take specific actions to be the steward of your future.

PERILS OF THE BLIND SPOT

It's an old saying that keeps getting said because it's true: "If you don't know where you're going, any road will take you there." Will you get lucky by letting the fates decide your career for you? You might. But should you allow your career to be based on luck? We don't advise it.

Neglecting to develop a strategic plan and establish interim goals will make it more difficult for you to take advantage of your strengths. The value of relying on strengths as you navigate your career should not be underestimated. It's true that you can learn new things and improve existing skills, but you have *inherent strengths*. Why not leverage your superpowers to help you design a meaningful career that will leave you feeling satisfied and fulfilled? When you think about setting goals, start with your strengths instead of reaching for something way outside your area of expertise. Our experience shows that using strengths to aid your career trajectory will get you farther much faster.

Lakshmi, who worked in a large insurance corporation, is a good example. One of her superpowers was creativity and problem-solving skills. Her bedside table always had an eclectic stack of books because she was curious and interested in learning. While she liked the company she worked for, she wasn't always that content in her assigned roles. Lakshmi continually found herself in process jobs that she easily could do because the work was mostly a matter of moving things along and hitting deadlines. But she was frustrated. She felt that her work rarely allowed her to employ her brainstorming skills, find inventive solutions to sticky problems, or showcase her creativity. She had a superpower that was covered over in burlap.

Once she established what was really important to her, she landed a job with a start-up. Her new job allowed her to help the company by using her finely honed process skills, and because the company was new, she had plenty of opportunities to use her creativity in ways that served the business.

Not being strategic in your career goals can also lead to a job that isn't closely aligned with or won't amplify your values or the things that are important to you. Alaine, for example, wanted a career based on public service, but she also wanted the better compensation that came with a job in the private sector. She knew that a nonprofit organization was unlikely to pay the salary she felt she needed to live comfortably. By being clear about the work she wanted to do and letting others know, she landed a role in her company's newly created initiative for sustainability. Alaine could contribute to the company, satisfy her passion for public service, and be compensated in the way that was important to her.

COACH ON YOUR SHOULDER
Questions to Help You Reflect on Where You Are Now

- What stories have you been telling yourself that could hold you back from creating or stating your long-term goals?
- What new story can you tell yourself and others about what you want to do next and into the future?
- How might you reframe your situation to see opportunities differently?
- What practical concerns might you need to take into account as you plan your career?
- If you have a plan, how can you refine it? Where can you get more specific about what you want?

- If you could do anything in your work or career and not fail, what would you do?
- How can you turn your dreams into reality?

STRATEGIES

Dedicate significant time to dreaming. Seriously—close your eyes, think about where you are, and then dream about what you want, where you want to land. One client told us that after spending considerable time dreaming, she realized that her main goal was not to have a boss. She made her dream come true by eventually starting her own business. A woman Brenda coached revealed her ambition: "I want to be one of the gods of executive board searches." Her goal was clear. After that, it was easier to plan how to get there. Here are time-tested strategies we've offered to our clients to help them figure out how to find their direction:

Assess Your Strengths, Weaknesses, Opportunities, and Threats

This exercise, called SWOT, is one CEOs do periodically for the companies they run, but you can also do it as an individual. Take stock of what is in your pantry.

STRENGTHS What do you do well, what skill sets do you have, what characteristics can you bring to bear? Are you a world-class project manager? Are you good at organizing or collaborating? Do you love to tackle and solve big, complex problems? What have you accomplished that you can talk to others about? What about your work brings meaning to your life? In what situations do you feel most confident?

WEAKNESSES What skill deficits do you have that might create obstacles to your career path? In which areas would you like to develop and grow? Have you received feedback about where you could improve? In which situations are you most likely to lack confidence?

OPPORTUNITIES What areas do you see that could benefit from improvement? How might you amplify your strengths? Where in the company might you look for fresh opportunities? Do you see market trends where you could use your skills and expertise in new ways?

THREATS What potential obstacles and challenges could block your progress? Are you starved for time? Are you working in an area that is losing market share or that is impacted by rapidly changing technology? What resources and other support will you need to achieve your vision?

Now write down what you've discovered. Figure 2 shows an example of what it might look like:

STRENGTHS	WEAKNESSES
I am creative. I have strong interpersonal and communication skills. I know technology. I am a driver; I make things happen. I love change. I am courageous.	I lack knowledge about all lines of business. I have narrow exposure across the company. My network is limited. I haven't established a specific strategy to achieve my goals.
OPPORTUNITIES	THREATS
My company has plans to expand and is working to grow new lines of business. I'm not afraid to ask for help. I can take courses offered by the company to expand my skills and competencies.	I need help to get key assignments to better learn the business. It will take time to build relationships. I need time to develop influence with decision-makers.

Figure 2. Example of a SWOT analysis

Scenario Planning

Many organizations employ a process called scenario planning that is designed to account for variables as they consider the future. For example, how would an escalation in gas prices, a pandemic, or a shortage of workers affect long-range business planning? Although no one ever has a crystal ball, the unknowns can be managed better if a company plans for different scenarios. This strategy also works for personal career planning because it helps you know how to pivot. Our research on successful women shows that women pivot in many different directions as they gather experience that takes them to their destination. Think through three or four different scenarios for your career. Try them on by asking: "Which scenario would work best now?" "What might you shift to if the situation changes?" "What needs to change so you can pivot the way you'd like to?"

Add to Your Informal Research

Do you like what you do and the company or business you work for? Talk to others who are knowledgeable about the company or business you are in. In which areas is the company investing? What do your colleagues or associates see happening in the marketplace? Are some parts of the business expanding? Are there areas that are struggling that could benefit from your knowledge or expertise? Where do you see your company going and what areas might provide good potential for growth?

Sometimes you might end up somewhere that doesn't suit you. In that case, you can talk to others in human resources, trade associations, industries, and jobs that interest you. These are called informational interviews. The idea is to learn more about those careers and roles so you can gauge your own interest and outlook.

Know the Job Market

As you talk to people, ask them to imagine where things are going in your company's field and any related industries you're interested in. What industries can expect to see growth? Based on the trends, what skill sets are companies looking for? Find out what your present company is looking for and consider whether it's a match with what you want to do long term. If it's not, what other industries might offer what you're more interested in?

Consider What You *Don't* Want

Sometimes it's easier to back into what you want by achieving clarity about things that you would not prefer. What have you done in the past that you don't want to continue? Are there conditions or environments you don't want to tolerate? Mull over the practical considerations, such as your financial needs or whether you're cut out for long commutes and lots of travel or, conversely, whether you have an aversion to being desk bound. Do you prefer to work from home? Is a family-friendly work environment important to you? These practical considerations can help you rule out certain paths.

Construct a Plan or Adapt to the Scenario of Your Choice

Visualize wide sky, then bring it down to the rooftops. What do you feel ready to commit to? Talk to people about the possibilities, then take notes. As the owner of your career, you need a vision of where you are going and a clear idea of the goals and actions that can help get you there. If this seems hard, it's because it is. Many women tell us, "I cannot set a plan because there are too many unknowns." Here's the good news: plans are just that. They can always be revised. You're not swearing an oath to a lifetime commitment. You're setting a direction that can be changed, adjusted, and fine-tuned as your career unfolds and life circumstances change.

Earn Your "Badges"

One of the leaders Kathryn worked with often said, "Go toward the goal. Learn the skills for the job you want, not the job you have." Research shows that growing your career is a mix of work experience (70 percent), interaction with others (20 percent), and formal education (10 percent). Once you've established a direction and a vision, you can concentrate on the 70 percent. What experience do you need? Think of it as earning badges, just as you would at a summer camp or for a digital credential. Assignments that force you to stretch will facilitate growth. This is more important than formal training programs. For example, Kathryn earned a "badge" in mergers and acquisitions. Brenda earned a "badge" in customer service turnaround. These badges become credentials for your reputation and the next level of work. Every level of leadership needs different skills, according to Michael Lombardo and Robert Eichinger, the authors of *The Leadership Machine*.[4] Basic management is about technical skills, planning, and organizing. Advanced management is about hiring staff, delegating, and negotiating. What skills do you need to get where you want to be? The title of career coach Marshall Goldsmith's book, *What Got You Here Won't Get You There*, offers a crucial insight.[5] If you want to get from the front line to the next level, what badges do you need to get there? If you don't know, ask and keep asking. Consider a lateral job move as a way of getting more or different experience or making new connections. Many of the successful women leaders we know made a lot of job changes on the way. This enabled them to grow more quickly.

Practice Articulating What You Want

Start by talking to a few trusted people about your dreams and goals and ask for their feedback so you can refine your message. Don't be afraid to be bold. In our coaching practice, we find that women veer toward safety instead of strong, direct, concise statements. We encourage you to be daring. Make statements such as "I want to lead people," "I am good at organizing and mentoring and I can grow talent," or "I'm known for building team spirit with staff." Think of it as "career college": declare your major, commit to it, and communicate your vision to others.

Find Your Connections

Who are the people you need to talk to or influence or who might be willing to help you? Make a clear ask: "This is what I'm looking for, this is what I need, and this is why I think it will help me be more effective." Ask people to help you meet others, get an assignment, or review an important document. Look for opportunities to make strategic connections in ways that reflect your authentic style. It's not about networking or "working the room"; it's about finding the people you can have a mutually beneficial relationship with. If people don't know what you want, as was the case for Corinna, they can't help. People want to help, so tell them what you want.

Kathryn was talking with a former coaching client she hadn't seen or talked to in some time. The woman delightedly reported to Kathryn that she had achieved her goal of becoming a chief operating officer partly by letting others know what she wanted and by developing relationships with people who could help. She also reported a new goal: to become the chief administrative officer of a Fortune 100 company. She was looking for a company that was big and established but was also going through a messy challenge so she could restore order from chaos, one of her major strengths. It was a bold dream, and she was busy developing strategies to make it come true.

STORIES THAT HOLD US BACK

Many women tell us they can't make a plan because they're unable to decide or they don't want to be boxed in. They have many reasons why they can't declare a "major" for their career. We're going to reiterate: make a plan, because you can always change it and most likely will. You can have a plan *for now*. It used to be that people had an average of three different jobs or careers over their lifetime in the workforce. Now it is more likely to have that many changes by midcareer, and this dynamic is likely to keep changing. Nowadays, people typically have several jobs or careers in their portfolios. The goal isn't to lock you in but rather to give yourself a direction to prevent drift.

We understand that sometimes the thought of wanting more, especially when you're juggling many aspects of life, can feel overwhelming. We had one client who likened her life to a carefully constructed house of cards. She was juggling childcare, taking care of elderly parents, and attending to her marriage. She had established a precarious work-life balance and worried that a promotion or an expanded role would be like trying to add another card to the house, causing the whole thing to collapse. But that doesn't have to be an obstacle to *planning*. Making a plan can enable you to be more mindful about pursuing the career that works for your life.

When we encourage women to be more deliberate about goals related to their career development, it doesn't often come naturally to them. They say things such as:

"I'm not sure of my next move; I can just go where they need me."

"I'm not sure whether I can do the big job."

"I can't decide what my long-term goal is."

"Even though others think I'm qualified, I don't want to apply. I don't think I am ready."

"I worry about what others would think of me if I said I wanted to be the CEO."

"I don't have time to work on my career. I have clients to serve and a family to take care of."

As we mentioned in the introduction, sometimes the voices in your head—those voices that chatter at you and sometimes try to convince you that "you're not all that"—can prevent you from being precise about what you want. If you believe what those voices are saying, you'll hesitate to go big. Don't allow the background noise to hold you back. Laura, a deputy CEO of a major consulting firm, says shutting down her inner critic was a key ingredient to her success.

Much has been written about imposter syndrome, the fear that you will be exposed for not knowing what you should know. It's a worry that despite your knowledge and skills, people will discover that you're actually a fraud. We see many examples of women whose career advancement is held up by a fear of speaking up or hesitating to ask for plum assignments. They don't apply for jobs or promotions unless they're confident that they know everything about how to do it. This can prevent the kind of learning you need to grow and advance. If taking on something bigger and better feels a little scary, that just makes you human. Having a little fear doesn't mean you can't do it. Don't let your limiting beliefs hold you back.

In coaching, we find that many women are overly loyal to their companies, their teams, or their manager. They can be too concerned about "leaving the house in order" before they take on a new role. While loyalty is a wonderful trait, if you allow that to be your driver, you might postpone the promotion because you have a project to finish or stay put because you can't imagine how your team will go on without you. It's important to know when it's time to move on or change things up. Don't let comfort or loyalty keep you from seeking new challenges.

THE POWER OF REFRAMING: A NEW STORY

Remember Corinna from earlier in this chapter? After she got over her surprise that people didn't know her career aspirations, Corinna began to self-reflect. She began examining her situation more closely and thinking about what she wanted. She talked to peers, colleagues, friends, and one of her old bosses about what she had learned about herself. Corinna began to take inventory of her strengths, analyzing where and how she could make her mark. She worked to quiet the negative voices in her head that had subconsciously contributed to a subtle embarrassment about wanting to get ahead.

After productive conversations with us and some of her colleagues and mentors, she began making what we call strategic asks. To get where she wanted to go, she needed to expand her knowledge and skills and earn "badges" by contributing to different work projects. She knew she needed to get assigned to key task forces and volunteer for relevant committees. Once she established a direction, she got her career wheels rolling. She was soon working with a key committee that gave her work exposure and helped her develop important contacts. Both developments moved her toward her goal and helped her understand what steps to take to earn even more "badges." She became known for being effective at managing change and shepherding challenging projects to completion. As she broadened her experience, she got noticed, and eventually she was asked to take over the account of a huge and important client.

An executive Brenda worked with often talked about the people who "couldn't see beyond their headlights." They can't see their potential or anything beyond what the headlights illuminated. They need to see more of their capabilities, see themselves in other capacities and not just where they are today. When she asked what that meant, he responded that such people couldn't see anything beyond their headlights and therefore weren't thinking about a long-range direction or imagining the possibilities that lay beyond what was right in front of them. His perspective was that they'd given up on believing that they could do more or imagining different possibilities and were therefore more likely to remain stuck.

What stories do you tell yourself that might be holding you back? As you become aware of them, write them down. Ask yourself, "Are these things true?" Then create a new story about yourself, one that sets intentions and helps you envision who you want to be and where you want to go.

Corinna thought that focusing on the work in front of her would get her noticed and that people would naturally ask her to take on more. Sometimes it works like that, but why not boost your chances by advertising your good work and telling people where you'd like it to take you?

Getting the job done is important, of course. But if you want to effectively manage your career, you need to develop goals and take strategic steps to achieve them. Look for the people who have the power to help you and let them know what you want. Work to influence others and seek ways to help others achieve their goals. As Corinna said to us, "I know a lot of people, but there are also a lot of people I don't know well. I need to find a way to create relationships with people who might be able to help me."

Ursula Burns, the former CEO of Xerox and the first Black CEO of a Fortune 500 company, has written a book about her career called *Where You Are Is Not Who You Are*.[6] In her discussion of what made her successful, she notes that her mother taught her many important lessons, including, "Don't let the world happen to you. You go out and happen to the world." This is what we want for you. Make a plan and happen to the world.

COACH ON YOUR SHOULDER
Tips for Steering Clear of the Blind Spot

MAKE YOU A PRIORITY Create a set period to think about or reassess your goals and outline the steps you're taking. Consider it a retreat for brainstorming and establishing your personal strategic initiatives. We are big proponents of blocking out time on your calendar and protecting that time for the purpose of consciously taking concrete actions that will further your career. If your calendar is reminding you of the importance of this task, it's harder to skip it or let it slide.

CREATE VISUAL REMINDERS A document or spreadsheet or even a vision board can become a tangible, visual reminder of your goals and the steps you intend to take to achieve them. Consider developing a spreadsheet that outlines the steps you need to take to manage your career. List the activities you intend to complete and give them a suggested due date. Make a column for the names of people who can help you in some way. Your career is a project, and a project needs management. Use the strategies you implement to be successful at work to help you achieve your career goals. Every month or so, return to the list and give yourself a grade.

SCHEDULE YOURSELF IN Make a lunch or coffee date with someone to talk about what you want. Tell the person that you have a specific agenda: to talk about your career. When your companion knows you have an agenda, it will give them time to think about how they can help. It will also give a focus to your conversation that is harder to back away from.

STEER YOUR CAREER It's essential to have a destination in mind, but like any journey, your career navigation is likely to include twists, turns, and detours. Stay flexible. You have a plan, but it's important to remember that even the best-laid plans need to be adjusted from time to time. If you find yourself unhappy in your job, remember that you want to steer *toward* something better, not away from something you don't prefer. Don't get stuck in the whirlpool of indecision. No decision *is* a decision.

BROADEN YOUR VISION INSEAD, the San Francisco–based international business school, reviewed thousands of 360-degree assessments over five years to see how women ranked in leadership abilities compared to men. In a *Harvard Business Review* article highlighting the findings, women got higher average ratings than men in most of the leadership dimensions measured. But there was one exception: women scored lower on "envisioning," the ability to recognize new opportunities and trends in the environment and develop new strategic directions.[7] Taking this task into account as you plan your career will boost your opportunity to stand out.

LEARN TO SAY "NO" GRACEFULLY You will be asked to do things or take assignments that will not fit your goal. Be thoughtful. Saying "no" to some things will allow you to say "yes" to more strategic things. Consider the three rules of saying no:

Give yourself the "gift of the gap." Ask for time to think about it before responding, but avoid using words like "maybe," which can be interpreted as a tepid yes.

Respond respectfully and in a way that maintains the relationship: "This role is exciting, but I want to complete the work on a project I've already committed to. Thank you for asking."

Offer a suggestion that might help—another person they could ask or a different strategy to consider. Introduce them to someone else who might help.

We know good leaders are outcome oriented and have a clear destination. Determine yours. You can always pivot and change—most of us do—but with a vision and set goals, your career will be on a well-thought-out path, just like any good business plan.

SUMMARY:
What We Want You to Know

- Create a vision for your career to avoid the risk of drifting and ending up in a role you don't find satisfying.

- Grow your skills for the job(s) you want.

- Assess your strengths, weaknesses, obstacles, and threats and get feedback from others about your work, the industry you want to work in, and the marketplace.

- Define and continually add to the portfolio of skills you will need to get to the next level.

- Create a long-term vision and smaller strategic goals. Go after the assignments, roles, and relationships that can help you achieve them.

- Think like a CEO—create a business plan for yourself.

- Be bold about letting other people know what your vision is and where you want to land.

CHAPTER TWO

Lack of Self-Awareness

Know Who You Are and How You Land with Others

Is this real? Or is it just happening inside my head?
Of course, it is happening inside your head, Harry.
Why should that mean that it's not real?

— J. K. ROWLING, *HARRY POTTER AND THE DEATHLY HALLOWS*

Lonni, who works for a large manufacturing company, stood her ground as the leadership team grilled her during a presentation. The discussion had turned confrontational, and Lonni, the only woman in the meeting, later told Kathryn: "The meeting felt like a rumble, and I was alone. I really felt like I was right and stood my ground, but there was no one else to defend me." At home that night, she couldn't shake her anxiety. She felt angry about the way some of her colleagues had argued with her and was worried that she had hurt or offended others with her insistence that she was correct. The meeting had left her feeling so unsettled that she couldn't sleep.

The next day, Lonni went into her office with high trepidation, uncertain about how she should act and how others would react when they saw her. As she walked through the hallway, one of her colleagues greeted her cheerfully and asked how she was doing. "Not great," she replied. Lonni told him how upset the meeting had left her and how she had spent a sleepless night ruminating about the disagreements. He looked surprised. "Hey, that wasn't about you," he said. "You shouldn't be taking this personally. We like working with you, we just didn't like your idea."

During a coaching session, Lonni admitted that she had let her thoughts get the better of her. After the meeting, she'd created a huge story in her head about how the leadership team didn't like her. She had told herself that they were out to get her and she'd never be able to sell them her ideas. "Why do you think that's the case?" Kathryn asked. Through more conversation, Lonni realized that her fears were rooted in her upbringing. She'd grown up in a family that avoided talking about hard things. Disagreements were dangerous and conflict was perilous. The voices in her head had been sending messages that if she disagreed with others, they would dislike her or would not want to work with her.

Lonni's awareness allowed her to reframe the way she viewed conflict and disagreement. Once she understood that a vigorous argument for her point of view didn't make her less likable, she learned to take a stand without taking disagreements personally. With practice, her newly discovered awareness allowed her to work with others in a more effective and productive way.

THE BLIND SPOT: THE ILLUSION OF SELF-AWARENESS

The tricky thing about self-awareness is that too often people convince themselves that they know more about themselves than they do. The challenge of self-awareness is finding ways to be *intentional* about knowing what your behavior, styles, and personality are and understanding their influence in the context of your interactions with others.

Here is our secret: the best, most effective leaders are self-aware. Research backs up this idea. A large-scale study done in 2018 by organizational psychologist Tasha Eurich and her team, for example, showed that self-awareness contributes to confidence, clear communication, creativity, better decisions, strong relationships, and business profitability.[1]

That's what many studies show. Unfortunately, Eurich's research also revealed that a self-aware person can be hard to find. "Even though most people believe they are self-aware, we estimate that only 10–15 percent of the people we studied actually fit the criteria," Eurich wrote.[2] We believe this means that the majority of leaders suffer from the illusion that they are self-aware, so they unconsciously let themselves off the hook of mindfully working to increase their self-awareness.

Talk about a blind spot!

In our coaching, we stress that self-awareness includes understanding that how you behave and how you "land" with others when they interact with you could be getting in your own way. Eurich's research touches on this. Her team defined two forms of self-awareness. The first is *internal*, which is based on how clearly you are able to define values, understand your reactions, and notice the ways you impact others. *External* self-awareness is the ability to understand how other people view you in the same way. The feedback we've heard over and over again in the thousands of feedback assessments we've done for women is this: "She doesn't really see how she comes off. She doesn't seem to understand how her style is getting in her way."

The two kinds of self-awareness are symbiotic. One feeds the other. Effective leaders, Eurich writes, are those who actively work on both "seeing themselves clearly and getting feedback to understand how others see them."[3]

Like Lonni, everyone has mental messages, endlessly looping tapes, and mental voices that chatter incessantly and insistently. Often those voices tell us stories that don't reflect reality. One of Kathryn's longtime mentors would often tell her with a chuckle, "You know what? We're all crazy. And the people who don't think they are crazy? They are the craziest of all." His advice? Make it a point to figure out your quirks, idiosyncrasies, peculiarities, and "craziness" so that you can learn to drive them instead of letting them drive you.

It's hard to quell those voices. They send counterproductive messages that tell us, in one way or another, "You're not good enough, you're not smart enough, you're not persuasive enough, you're not that likable." The negativity goes on and on. Conversely, your stories can make you overly self-assured to the point that you are blind to the ways your actions negatively affect others and you feel impervious to the need for help and input. Listening closely to those mental voices is important because they have the power to keep you from being successful. If you examine your internal stories closely, you'll typically see that they aren't reflecting reality.

The great news is that self-awareness can be acquired, and it doesn't require therapy. (We're not knocking therapy. That can be a great way to develop self-awareness.) With a measure of curiosity, humility, and willingness to try something different, plus some hard work and perseverance, you can change what's not working for you.

The development of self-awareness is often made more difficult because it tends to inspire deep feelings of vulnerability—not the most comfortable emotion to experience. But as Dr. Brené Brown, the author of *Daring Greatly* and *The Gifts of Imperfection*, says, "Vulnerability sounds like truth and feels like courage. Truth and courage aren't always comfortable, but they're never weaknesses. . . . Courage starts with showing up and letting ourselves be seen."[4] Embracing vulnerability is necessary for maximizing the benefits of self-awareness, which will help you see reality more clearly, put those voices in their place, and create a more useful and productive perspective about who you really are.

Effective leaders understand that awareness is the first, essential step to change. You can't alter what you can't see and what you don't know. Analyzing your faulty thoughts and stories is the first step toward allowing you to govern them more consistently and effectively. Once you're aware of how you land with other people, you'll be better able to make corrections and adjustments to increase your confidence and influence.

PERILS OF THE BLIND SPOT

One of our co-workers, Jae, is bright, competent, and a hard charger. She is liked and respected by her colleagues and her clients. Her evil twin is another story. Kathryn remembers the day Jae confided that her "ugly twin sister" had made an appearance at a high-stakes meeting where Jae was feeling stressed and under pressure. "What do you mean?" Kathryn asked, a little confused. Jae laughed. "What you might not realize is that I have a dark side that I call my evil twin sister. Sometimes she takes over my body and says things I would never say and does things I would never do." In those moments, Jae says, it feels like she is no longer in control of her words and actions. Later, when she comes back to herself and realizes she has a big mess to clean up, she jokes with others that her "evil twin" took over. Sometimes Jae would tell Kathryn with a sigh, "I had to write another apology note today."

While Jae knew that her strengths as a driver and a leader who demanded excellence served her well, she also recognized that those qualities got diluted when her behavior, tone, and language erupted in a way that put people off. Her jokes about her evil twin would only take her so far, and Jae was determined to find strategies that would lead to new ways of being. She tapped into her inner observer and paid close attention to the signals her body gave her in situations that triggered the appearance of her "evil twin." When her fists began to clench or she began holding her breath or her heartbeat kicked into a higher gear, she knew it was time to take a long, deep breath or a short break so she could regain control. A mindful pause enabled her to step back into the kind of leader she intended to be.

Michael Lombardo and Richard Eichinger's *Career Architect Development Planner* outlines a career derailer called the "blocked personal learner."[5] The traits of someone who is bound to get stalled in their personal growth include:

Not insightful about herself

Lacks curiosity

Closed to new skills, approaches, and tactics

Prefers staying the same even when faced with new information

These characteristics are career derailers. People who do not self-reflect, actively seek feedback, and try new approaches will become stuck. They're far more likely to get stalled in their careers and to be far less effective in their roles. One of our clients, a C-suite leader for a technology company, had often been told that she was "way too hard on people." Her hard-driving and exacting management style had contributed to her promotion to a high level in the organization. Unfortunately, instead of using those qualities judiciously, she had let them take over. Her reputation had become a big problem, and many colleagues and prospective hires had begun saying they weren't willing to work with her or for her. "I need to find a way to back it down," she told Brenda. "I don't want to drive away quality people because I'm perceived as too hard to work for."

A great strength allowed to run amok can trip you up. When you wield your strength like a sword in battle, people are going to defend themselves instead of being open to your input and ideas. Developing self-awareness about whether you're using your strengths in the best possible way will help you avoid the trap that our client Deidre found herself in. As a college athlete, she had succeeded at the highest levels because of her discipline and love of competition. She was motivated to be "the winner." While her love of competition served her well in the sales organization where she worked, it began to backfire when she got feedback that she was even competing against her own colleagues, to the detriment of the business. "My big advantage has become a disadvantage," Deidre told Brenda. She asked for help to channel some of that competitive energy into collaboration and teamwork.

In the same week, we heard from another client, Thea, who told us she'd received feedback that she constantly one-upped people at the real estate company where she worked. Her colleagues found it annoying and off-putting. After a few key questions and some self-reflection, Thea said she thought the bad habit had its roots in her childhood. She grew up in a family that wasn't poor, exactly, but was always on the edge. She was a decent student, but her grades were nothing to brag about. Because she often felt insecure, she felt compelled to tell people she was "cool enough, and smart enough" as a way of reassuring herself and others that she belonged. She learned that her style and the way others reacted to it was getting in the way of her ability to succeed. Once she realized she was turning off the very people she wanted to see her as competent and likable, Thea went to work on toning down her tendency to outshine others.

The role of feedback in developing self-awareness and behavior change is essential, and it's especially important that women not be passive about seeking it. You don't have to wait for your annual review. In fact, you most definitely shouldn't.

One reason? A *Harvard Business Review* article published in September 2021 suggests that women should ask for feedback frequently because they're less likely to get it than men are.[6] In addition, research shows that although women are just as likely as men to *ask* for feedback, they are less likely to get specific, actionable feedback than men are. And it's not just your boss you should be asking; it's also useful to solicit specific feedback in conversations with colleagues, vendors, customers, and other stakeholders. When you have work-related conversations with colleagues or supervisors, ask questions about how what you do ties to business outcomes and professional accomplishments or what you could do differently to improve work relationships.

It's especially important for women to be very specific about what they ask for. A different *Harvard Business Review* article about self-awareness and women focuses on a study showing that even when women ask for feedback, they are less likely to get it, and if they do get it, it's so general that it's not helpful.[7] The article points out a variety of reasons for this, but the bottom line is that if women aren't getting *actionable* feedback, it can stunt their growth. When you're told you're "a good team player" or your presentation "went well," follow up with questions that give you something to chew on. Here are some ways to get the kind of feedback that will truly help you: "What team-building skills do you see as being particularly useful in this job?" "What did you find most impactful about the presentation?" "Thanks for the kind words, but what is one thing you would suggest I could do to improve?"

COACH ON YOUR SHOULDER
Questions to Help You Reflect on Where You Are Now

- What messages do you hear when you listen to the voice and the stories in your head?
- What do you hear that might be holding you back?
- How would it be possible for you to have a different view of yourself?
- What new stories do you need to create?
- Who can you identify that can give you insights and increase your self-awareness?
- How often do you ask for feedback? What do you do with the feedback you get?

STRATEGIES

Self-awareness presents a bit of a conundrum in the sense that many people assume that they are already self-aware. This can stop them from actively developing self-awareness. Cultivating this important characteristic can be like trying to land a job when you have no experience. True self-awareness needs a big dose of humility, keen observation, and the deliberate pursuit of feedback. What follows are the strategies we suggest to our coaching clients.

Conduct Your Own 360 Assessment

The most successful leaders, as rated by 360-degree reviews of leadership effectiveness, seek frequent critical feedback from bosses, peers, employees, and board members. Not only does feedback make you more self-aware, the very act of asking for it can make others perceive you as more effective. When you're the one soliciting feedback, it also mitigates the instinctive defensiveness most people feel when they receive unsolicited feedback. According to behavioral statistician Joseph Folkman, "The very act of asking for feedback puts you in a better position to listen carefully to the feedback, ask clarifying questions, and then accept the remarks."[8]

One woman we know, Suzanne, has a practice of sitting down every year with several colleagues, clients, and other stakeholders in her industry to ask specific questions about things she should begin doing, stop doing, and continue doing. She keeps the group manageable; it is a small but significant group of folks she trusts to deliver honest assessments and who know her well enough for the feedback to be useful. Some of the people in her feedback group are regulars. (When Suzanne shows up in their offices, they say, "Are you going to ask me those questions again?") But she also tries to include a few new people each year.

When we asked Suzanne what she got out of her practice, she replied, "I don't want to drive blind. I come away with a sense of what people think I'm good at and I get good advice about what I need to do to be more effective." We will be talking more about the critical importance of getting good, real-time feedback from others and ways to do it in chapter 4.

Personality Assessments

Personality assessments are another good tool that provide insight about how you're wired and how that might affect the ways you interact and communicate with others. Common assessments include the Myers-Briggs Type Indicator, StrengthsFinder, the DiSC assessment (which identifies dominance, influence, steadiness, and conscientiousness), the Hogan Personality Inventory, the Riso-Hudson Enneagram Type Indicator, and the Positive Intelligence Program. Many are available in some form online at no cost. These tools are designed to reveal your preferences and styles and help you to understand your innate ways of being. They also can be useful in helping you influence others if you understand and can speak to their personalities, perspectives, and preferences. These preferences are strong, which is a good reason to be aware of them and pay attention to them. They help you see how you're wired to function. If you lack knowledge about how these powerful, innate ways of being operate in interactions with other people, you may find that you're not as effective at work as you could be.

Develop and Demonstrate Confidence

Working with women on confidence is a big chunk of our coaching work—and one of the reasons we emphasize preparation and practice as a way to build and boost it. (We write about this in detail in chapter 5.) In *Break Your Own Rules*, Kathryn and her coauthors offered a list of confidence markers.[9] They are revealed in the following physical behaviors:

Posture: Stands full height, feet under shoulders, with balance and relaxed energy.

Speaking volume and tone: Varies appropriately for content but stays mostly in the moderate range; avoids ending sentences with a lowered or questioning tone.

Muscular language: Uses words, adverbs, and phrases that emphasize certainty or self-assurance; uses vocabulary to ensure that meaning and nuance are conveyed.

Through our coaching, we have seen too many cases of women who are exceedingly competent but haven't found ways to exude confidence or personal presence. Kathryn remembers a colleague sharing that she was consistently being told, "You need to be confident." She asked her boss, "What's the deal?" He replied: "If you're not confident, it's a reflection on you—and me." One time, Kathryn was in a three-way online meeting with a client and her boss and watched as the client twirled her hair, flipped her pen like a baton, and fidgeted in her chair. Kathryn was able to send her a private message about how distracting those behaviors were in that setting and how they made her appear nervous and less confident. The woman stopped and gained her focus and composure for the rest of the meeting. Tune in to the times you are giving away your power and work hard to change those behaviors.

Find Your Sense of Humor

Laugh about the crazy things the voices in your head say about you and your limiting beliefs. We are funny creatures; we might as well find a way to chuckle at our foibles. Our colleague, Diana, is a strong extrovert who is aware that she talks a lot. Sometimes she pauses and begins to giggle, and then says, "Hey, I know this is a hard issue, and my way is to talk all this through out loud because that's the way extroverts think." Sometimes, she just uses shorthand: "Excuse me, I'm just extroverting again." She exhibits authentic vulnerability about something she is self-aware about, and it works. Vulnerable people aren't weak—they are powerful.

Break a Pattern

Separating yourself from the task at hand or a situation gives you space to think more clearly and make an attitude adjustment. Research shows that even short breaks can heighten your ability to focus and improve performance.[10] In a study that used a computer application to track workers' work habits, researchers came across an unexpected finding: the most productive employees were those who took the most breaks. Calling a time-out also can be useful for defusing tense situations. It's OK to say, "I can feel myself tensing up and getting defensive, and that's not productive. How about we take a breather and resume this conversation later?" Then reflect on or ask for feedback about what you might have done differently in that situation.

Beware the Double Bind

Unfortunately, women continue to have to navigate gender stereotypes that can put them in double binds. Catalyst, a global nonprofit that works to advance and support women-friendly workplaces, refers to the dilemma for women as "damned if you do, doomed if you don't."[11] When women take charge (by delegating or solving problems), for example, they are viewed as competent but are seen as less likable. When women take care (by supporting others and rewarding subordinates), they are seen as less capable but tend to be well liked. Although it's unfair, what is seen as a positive trait in a male can be perceived as a flaw or a misstep for women. Tho Bella Dinh-Zarr, a former vice-chair and acting chairperson of the National Transportation Safety Board, has deep experience with the double bind. She has written about situations where she was told that she was pushy and interruptive when she interjected comments at meetings to set the record straight or redirect the conversation. When her male colleagues did the same thing, they were seen as "having something important to say."[12] We wish this double bind didn't create such a Catch-22 for women, but until the world has more women leaders, it's important to be aware of it, call it out, and be strategic about managing it.

STORIES THAT HOLD US BACK

Begin a practice of actually listening to the voices in your head. What are they saying to you and how might they be getting in your way? Women often tell us that those voices often say things like this:

"I don't really belong here."

"They just don't get me."

"I am not smart enough."

"Why should I have to change? They should accept me for who I am."

"I have high standards. If other people can't live up to them, it's not my problem."

These voices will assert themselves no matter where you are in your career, no matter how high your leadership position. For example, executives Jane Edison Stevenson and Evelyn Orr, who interviewed fifty-seven female CEOs, found that only five of the women had had a concrete goal of becoming a CEO.[13] Two-thirds of them said they didn't realize that becoming a CEO was possible until someone else told them. And eight said they didn't realize they wanted to be a CEO until after someone offered them the position. Their voices were telling them that women don't become CEOs.

Your self-image is a combination of what you think of yourself and what others think of you. Pay attention to the latter, too. Magdalena was considered a strong candidate for the CEO role of a national nonprofit organization. Other people in the organization, respected colleagues, were telling her she was ready, but the voices in her head argued that she wasn't. When we asked what was holding her back, she replied: "Fear, I guess fear. I am afraid I won't be successful." She couldn't see what others saw or hear that others were telling her that "you *are* ready."

Examining the underlying assumptions that arise from your voices and those of others is important. When one executive we worked with was accepted into Harvard's MBA program, her mom told her: "But people like us don't go to Harvard." She put that limiting belief aside and chose a new story that said, "I can do this." She went on to complete her Harvard degree and become a respected leader in her industry and an advocate for women leaders. She has authored several books and is a national platform speaker. "Thank goodness I didn't listen," she says.

Pay attention to the voices—both internal and external—and think hard about how they might be creating unnecessary obstacles. Not only is it important to become aware of what they're saying to you, it's also paramount for you to work on new messaging.

And if the voices are telling you to go for it, that is worth paying attention to as well, even if it makes you feel a little vulnerable.

THE POWER OF REFRAMING: A NEW STORY

Leesa is one of the most organized clients we've worked with. As a project manager for a large healthcare organization, she loves to create buttoned-up processes that are documented and signed off on. She keeps an epic to-do list and gets a great feeling of satisfaction from crossing off each accomplished task. She once confided, with a self-deprecating chuckle, that her closet is organized by color and her cooking spices are in alphabetical order.

While managing a large change project at work, she noticed that she was becoming increasingly impatient and frustrated with colleagues who peppered her with questions at every meeting. She said it was a constant stream of "What about this? What about that?"

Leesa felt like every question opened a fresh can of worms that distracted from the work she wanted to get accomplished. She wanted to check tasks off of her project to-do list. "I am constantly scrambling to get the worms back into a can instead of getting the necessary work done," she told us. When Kathryn asked why Leesa found the questions so frustrating—and why the situation had her feeling so down— she paused to reflect for a few moments. "I guess I just don't like chaotic, disorganized things," Leesa said. "When people ask me all these questions, I start feeling like everything is out of control."

She paused again, shaking her head as a lightbulb went off.
"Actually, I guess I just need to flip my script and get over it,"
Leesa said. "I know it is part of being human to ask questions.
I need to get better at telling myself a new story so that when
people ask questions or want more information, I can see that
they are just trying to get on board. And that is a good thing.
I've tended to see them as resisting, but really, they are just
asking good questions. I could choose to see that as them trying
to be helpful." Her insight helped lower her frustration and
improved her interactions with her colleagues.

Think about situations that get you going in an unproductive direction and examine the message in your head—the limiting belief. How could you create a more effective and encouraging message? For example, a lot of women say the voices are telling them, "I am not smart enough," which is a hard thing to admit—talk about vulnerability!

Human beings are not logical, they're psychological. How self-aware do you think you are on a scale of 1 to 10? What limiting beliefs can you identify? Here is an exercise that might help you develop additional self-awareness. Start by identifying two situations in which you feel uncomfortable, and then ask yourself these questions:

What is holding me back?

What will it take to move myself forward?

What do I need to do differently?

How could it be possible to see myself differently or create messages that are positive and productive?

Use the following form to explore answers to the questions and ways to reframe the messages that could be holding you back:

Directions: Think of two situations in which you are usually uncomfortable. List the stories that arise in your head in these situations and create a new story. See the example below in figure 3. Then list your own stories in figure 4.

SITUATION	STORY THAT HOLDS ME BACK	NEW STORY
You are in an annual promotion cycle.	"It's bad to talk about yourself. It's better to have people find out good things about me."	"If I don't tell them, they may never know."
Wait to help a prospective client on a project.	"If I call back, they'll think I'm pushy."	"If I call back, they'll think I'm interested in helping them."

Figure 3. Examples of stories that hold us back

SITUATION	STORY THAT HOLDS ME BACK	NEW STORY

Figure 4. Stories that hold us back worksheet

COACH ON YOUR SHOULDER
Tips for Steering Clear of the Blind Spot

GATHER YOURSELF Zara, a woman we coached, created a ritual she called "Gathering Myself." Every morning, she reviewed her schedule and thought about the ways she wanted to show up for each interaction. She set intentions about how she might respond if there were tension points or things didn't go the way she thought they should. At the end of the day, she spent a few minutes doing an "after-action review" to see how well she had lived out her intentions. You could do this on a morning commute or over your first cup of coffee or make it a weekly practice the evening before a new work week begins. Zara told us she can always tell when she skips her gathering practice, because when she reflects at the end of the day, she realizes she didn't handle things as well as she wanted to.

This is a form of meditation, a practice we believe is profoundly important. The length of time spent doing this is not as important as the quality of the effort and the act of doing so. Meditation helps center and focus on intentions and prepares us to have a purposeful impact on the world around us.

BEWARE OF THE IMPACT OF STRESS It's not uncommon for bad habits or unproductive behaviors to emerge when you're feeling under pressure. That is the time when your "evil twin" might want to assert herself. As one of our friends says, "No matter how many languages you learn, when you hit your thumb with a hammer, you swear in your native tongue." Kathryn's husband says he can tell when she's under stress because she starts cleaning closets to get her sense of control back. It's better than unloading on someone else, but it's still a distraction from her work. When you see or feel the signs of stress coming on, take a breath or take a break. Do some self-reflection and some self-talk. Kathryn tells herself,

"I am good at organizing things, but I don't need to be doing that right now." A strength can become a weakness if it's overused. Doing something you're used to might feel good, but it likely won't resolve your issue.

TAKE A CONSCIOUS BREATH After Kathryn shared a work dilemma with her daughter one day, her daughter said, "Mom, most of your problems could be solved just by taking a slow breath." It's good advice. In the book *Yoga Wisdom at Work*, Maren Showkeir and Jamie Showkeir point out that deep breathing has beneficial physiological effects. Deep breaths circulate more oxygen through the body and into the brain and can help you step back from the moment to find your inner observer in a way that facilitates clearer thinking. Mindful breathing "allows you to decelerate when you're feeling overwhelmed and stressed. It can calm an agitated or angry mind." Research shows that the pause offered by a few slow breaths calms your nervous system, which provides space to be intentional.[14] Your best self has more time to show up.

DON'T HIT SEND Be self-aware enough to know you need to step back. Be hypervigilant about taking action when you're in a reactionary mode. Don't send emails or texts or other written content when you're feeling angry—it never goes well. If it helps to create a draft to let off steam and make yourself feel better, fine, but don't press the send button! Emails are great for deciding where to have dinner or set a date for a meeting, not for resolving difficult issues.

KNOW WHEN TO HAVE THE CONVERSATION Speaking of email and texts, if you need to say no to someone, pick up the phone and have a conversation. Find a way to be gracious. Getting a no is almost always disappointing, and you need to be able to convey emotion, context, and grace with your tone. Many people prefer texts because it feels faster and a step removed, but we've seen far too many situations that have escalated out of control because tone is almost impossible to discern in email and texts. Even if you're a great writer, it's difficult to communicate about sticky situations that can generate nuanced feelings. Have a conversation.

KNOW WHEN TO MOVE CLOSER If you have relationship issues with a colleague, move toward them, not away. Your tendency might be to distance yourself from someone you don't like or trust and tell yourself stories about what you think they believe. They are likely doing the same about you. It's better to approach them and, as Stephen R. Covey writes about in *The Seven Habits of Highly Effective People*, "seek to understand."[15] As you climb in your career, learning the ways that others can be influenced is an essential skill. Doing that requires you to understand the perspectives of others, including how they see the world and what's important to them.

PERSIST Sometimes asking for what you need or trying to influence someone's decision or opinion fizzles. If it didn't go the way you had it planned in your head, try again. Develop a different strategy or approach and make another attempt. Build a business case for what you want. What's the worst that can happen? Maybe you'll get another no, but if nothing else, others will see you are persistent or have strong convictions. The other possibility? You just might be persuasive enough to get a yes.

FOSTER RESILIENCE Resilience is an essential characteristic for a leader. This became especially evident during the COVID-19 pandemic that began in 2020. Disappointing circumstances can often invite the "evil twin" to appear. But if you didn't get the promotion you wanted or your idea is rejected, you don't need to advertise in the moment how hurt and disappointed you are. Resist the temptation to say something you could regret. Try something we call In-the-Moment Resilience. First, take a deep breath. Second, find your "resting resilience face," a neutral expression that doesn't betray the churning emotions you might be experiencing. Get your outward self to project calm and confidence so that you are more likely able to communicate what needs to be communicated. If you can't get there in the moment, suggest that the topic be discussed at a later time, ask for a break, or prepare a statement for yourself in advance that you can use in these situations.

Brenda remembers a friend of hers who used a phrase over and over again: "Pay attention. This is big!" We'll repeat it here: Pay attention. Self-awareness is BIG. Use these strategies and coaching tips and figure out your new stories.

We are lighting the broom to clearly illuminate the importance of self-awareness. Don't fall into the illusion that you already know who you are. We can't emphasize this enough: *increasing your self-awareness will be a lifelong endeavor.*

SUMMARY:
What We Want You to Know

- Remember that good leaders are self-aware and that self-awareness is developed with intention and work.
- Cultivate self-awareness and remember that it is a lifelong journey. The sooner you begin, the farther and faster you'll go.
- Don't let your inner voices hijack your thoughts.
- Invest time in self-reflection. Think about interactions that didn't go the way you would have liked and formulate a plan for a new strategy.
- Get feedback from others about how your work habits, styles, and personality land with others. Resist the temptation to get defensive. Instead, be curious.

- Create a new story based on the person you want to be in the world.
- Identify specific practices that might help you be more intentional in your actions, especially in challenging circumstances.

CHAPTER THREE

Vague Reputationality

Get Known for Something and Tell Your Story

Figure out who you are and do it on purpose.

—DOLLY PARTON

What do people get when they get you?

We believe they get two things: the blend of what you do and who you are as a person. What you *do* establishes your reputation; who you *are* differentiates you from other people. Women should understand what they bring to the workplace and be able to talk about it authentically at a moment's notice. When personality attributes intersect with strong credentials, powerful things can happen.

Several foundational questions can help you see what you stand for and what makes you distinct in the world of work. What are you known for in your workplace? What do you want to be known for? What do people call you for and why do they call *you* instead of someone else? Do you know what people say about you when you're not in the room?

The last question is particularly important. If you don't know what people are saying, you won't have the ability to manage their perception of you. (And if you think managing perceptions is either impossible or unimportant, we can tell you it is very possible and it is very important.)

The answers to these questions are what the professional world refers to as your *brand*. Vague branding is one of the universal themes that emerge with women we coach. They consistently say: "I don't really have a brand." But if you're working with people, you have a reputation, even if it's "no one really knows what she does."

While brand is a utilitarian word, we prefer a term that combines the words "reputation" and "personality"—*reputationality*. Here's why: we know that women want to represent themselves in an authentic way. They care about being true to their core being and values. Reputationality is a blending of this core being and what you're known for professionally. And here is another truth: we are all known for something, whether it's what we do or how we do it or both. Your focus should be on making sure that what you're known for is what you want to be known for.

Both reputation and personality can work together to support the narrative a woman wants her colleagues to know about her. Reputationality is about authenticity; being known for who you truly are and your professional credentials and capabilities.

As soon as you set foot on your career path, investing mindful energy into developing, defining, and evolving your reputationality will be a career accelerator. You will benefit from keeping a consistent eye on this ball because your brand is never static. See figure 5, showing the dynamic nature of how your reputation and personality are continuously evolving. As your career progresses, you should be evolving, and so should your brand and your stories. It's important for you to constantly attend to this.

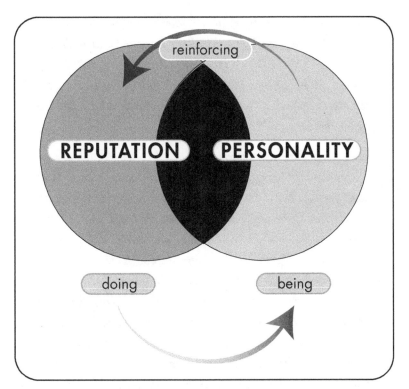

Figure 5. Reputationality

This means constantly learning about re-creating and reinventing your capabilities and your message as you advance. Many successful women executives we have coached and interviewed through the years have said that having a clear, strong brand is an advantage that leads to advancement or more opportunities.

> *Colleen, a new manager in a national consulting firm, was lucky to get a lesson early in her career about reputationality and the importance of knowing how to tell her story in a strong, prepared way at a moment's notice. One day, she dialed in early to a conference call and was first on the line. Putting the phone on mute, she began multitasking, intending to knock a few things off her to-do list while she waited.*

After a few moments, Paul, a senior manager, came on the line and introduced himself. Colleen unmuted and told Paul her name, "Oh, Colleen!" Paul said. "Someone suggested I get you on the new project I'm leading. While we're waiting for the others, why don't you tell me about yourself and what you do for the company?"

The project Paul was referring to was big, with ample learning and leadership opportunities. Colleen knew it could open doors for her. She wanted that assignment, and here was an unexpected opportunity to sell herself to the project leader! Unfortunately, she was unprepared and flustered. She began to ramble about some of the things she had worked on in the past, desperately trying to remember the things that would be relevant to the project. She knew she wasn't being clear and nothing she said was particularly memorable, which made her even more tongue tied. After a few moments Paul interrupted: "I've heard you're good at project management, and we could use that." He proceeded to talk about the project until the call began.

Colleen was frustrated because she wanted to be known for more than just her project management skills. She knew how to handle complex problems and work with difficult stakeholders. She had a wealth of experience, far beyond what Paul seemed to know about. But after the meeting began, she knew she had lost a valuable opportunity to tout her accomplishments, position herself in a memorable way, and emphasize her desire to be on the project team.

Although Colleen eventually was assigned to the project in a minor role, she lived with a big regret about not giving Paul a strong impression of her past performance and her relevant capabilities. She vowed she would never be caught unprepared again.

With coaching, she prepared a powerful set of messages and practiced delivery in a variety of scenarios and settings until she felt prepared and confident. She worked on two particular aspects of her reputationality—her innovative thinking and her ability to collaborate with stakeholders. She told us that her new messages made a positive difference in how others saw her expertise and opened up fresh opportunities.

We encourage women to think about whether the reputation they have is the one that they want. Does it represent who they are and what they stand for? Does it serve their goals and aspirations? Does it summarize and frame the best of who they are with the best of what they do? This takes deliberate, focused effort. It requires setting aside time for deep reflection as a means of getting clear and confident about what you want to put out into the world on purpose.

Many clients tell us that "personal brand" sounds contrived and disconnects them from their strong desire to be authentic. The best brands are built on authenticity, so we get it. It's one of the reasons we talk about reputationality. Cultivating your reputationality with authenticity and enthusiasm is a great way to distinguish yourself in a crowded workplace or marketplace. It can open doors and give you influence.

Getting clear about your intangible, essential assets leads to the next imperative—creating communication strategies that intentionally promote key messages about who you are to others who need to know. This isn't something many women feel comfortable doing. But as marketing and brand guru Steuart Henderson Britt says: "Doing business without promotion and advertising is like winking at [someone] in the dark. You know what you're doing— but nobody else does."[1] That's why we invest so much coaching time and energy in helping women promote themselves and the value they bring to others. We have seen the big impact it can make on a deliberate career.

BLIND SPOT: NOT KNOWING WHAT YOU'RE KNOWN FOR

Many of the women back away from the term "brand," which originated in marketing. It feels like a close relative to bragging, something most women are reluctant to do. Too many women believe that their good work will speak for itself, but that assumption is a big blind spot.

Women's reluctance to talk about what they do can be another of those double binds. Women are often socialized to believe that boasting is "unbecoming," and research shows they can be penalized even for exuding too much confidence. Data from a global technology company found that confident men were seen as having more influence in the organization, whereas women's confidence is viewed as acceptable only when it is combined with a "high prosocial orientation or the motivation to benefit others."[2] Women and men were treated differently for the appearance of self-confidence. Meghan I. H. Lindeman, Amanda M. Durik, and Maura Dooley, who surveyed over 200 college women, found that their subjects were uncomfortable with the idea of "self-promoting" because of perceived negative social consequences.[3]

We see this phenomenon in the women we work with. They often tell us that it feels distasteful to talk overtly about accomplishments, milestones, value-added work, and compliments from clients. They worry that doing so could be perceived as boasting or engaging in a crass form of workplace politics. One woman we coached said, "I've worked here a long time, and it seems like they should know what I do by now. Why is it my job to tell them?" However, what leaders tell us is that they rarely hear from employees or leaders in their organizations about what they are doing, the impacts they are having, or the value they are creating. Leaders and bosses are not mind readers. It is a mistake to rely on the belief that they do, in fact, know what you are doing.

The woman we were coaching was very clear about the excellence of what she was doing. It's also very likely that no one else was.

The secret to having authentic conversations about your impact is figuring out what you really do; crafting the stories that illustrate your skills, experience, and accomplishments; and then finding opportunities to have conversations in ways that won't come off as boastful or arrogant. We've seen many of our most successful clients do this with great effect.

Personal branding and marketing—reputationality—are essential to career management in the same way that they're critical to launching a product or service. The same disciplines apply: do market research, know what differentiates you from others, understand the audience, hone the message, build awareness, advertise, and get feedback from the marketplace about how you're doing.

Knowing who you are and achieving clarity about your key messages also helps you say yes to the right things and no to things that would distract you from your main purpose. When it is done well, your reputationality work can help others understand what's important to you and the kind of work you aspire to do.

PERILS OF THE BLIND SPOT

In our decades of doing thousands of feedback assessments for women, regardless of where in the world they work, we have rarely heard a readily available, clear, and concise statement from a woman about her reputationality. Women typically are unable to define their personal brand and rarely have a sense of how essential it is. And since they don't understand the importance of reputationality, they can't connect it to the importance of communicating it to others. The biggest danger here is that if you're not working to define yourself, others will define your reputation without your knowledge or consent.

Sometimes we've seen assessments that reveal a mismatch between a woman's reputation and how she wants to be perceived in the world. Aliyah, an up-and-coming senior leader in the financial industry, for example, was a rare client who had done the work and knew her reputationality. When we asked, she quickly and concisely stated that she was known as a fixer. In her organization, when a team or division had challenges or a product rollout needed substantial attention, folks called Aliyah. Although this reputation had served her well for many years, she wanted more and she wanted something different. She had evolved. Her career goals were no longer centered on fixing problems. She wanted to contribute in bigger and better ways, and she recognized that she needed a new brand that matched her evolution. She knew she had to craft and tell different stories to get her to where she wanted to go next.

Throwing a spotlight on what we do and the value we create helps others see this more clearly. Leaders are not all-knowing, and like all of us, they are wrapped up in their own work. You can't assume that they're going to look around to see and truly understand the valuable contributions of those around them. If you're not actively working on your reputationality, there is a danger that your good work will go unnoticed, and that can keep the doors of opportunity from opening up.

COACH ON YOUR SHOULDER
Questions for Reflection on Where You Are Now

- What three words describe what you want to be known for?
- What do you imagine people say about you when you're not in the room?

- Who do you want calling you and for what?
- How could your story become more powerful with the addition of data and details?
- How well is your brand reflected in social media, professional networks, your résumé, and your bio?
- When was the last time you revisited your reputationality? Does it reflect your current aspirations?
- If you had to reinvent yourself, what would you need to do?

STRATEGIES

Think of this in terms of a play that you're an actor in. You have a great deal of control over how you play your role and how the audience will perceive you. Celebrities and athletes have become skilled at building personal brands by being conscious and active about what they present to the public. With the rise of social media, you have even more ways to step onto a variety of "stages" and more opportunities to expand your brand and influence beyond your workplace. Authenticity is key to succeeding in your role. As David McNally and Karl Speak write in their book *Be Your Own Brand*, "Your brand is a perception or emotions maintained by somebody other than you."[4]

> *Naomi, an up-and-coming manager in a large consulting firm, got a feedback assessment with all-too-familiar themes. Although she was well liked, people could not define exactly what she did or the value she added to the business—a classic brand problem. She needed to get famous for something and she went to work on doing that.*
>
> *Like so many people, Naomi was in the habit of tossing out superficial answers to casual questions such as: "How's it going?" Her typical response was: "I am crazy busy. How are*

you?" Naomi realized she was missing opportunities to repre-sent her capabilities—and therefore her reputationality—in a more meaningful way. She wanted to answer the question in a way that would illuminate what she was working on or would let people know what she cared about. She began formulating concise points that would give specific shape and color to why she was "crazy busy" and how her work contrib-uted to her team and company. She tailored her response to the person asking the question and practiced enough that her answers sounded natural, authentic, and strong.

One day, she had a few minutes before the meeting started to chat with an influential partner in the firm. When the part-ner asked, "How's it going?" Naomi made it count. She said, "Lately I've been investing time with a tech client who just signed a $2 million statement of work with us. I'll be final-izing the project team next week. How are things with you?" The conversation with that partner continued after the call, who now had a better sense of Naomi and her work. Simple, quick, and powerful.

Here are strategies we've recommended to clients, who have used them to build their reputationality.

Take an Inventory

Begin by taking note of your specialty or niche, accomplishments, talents, and strengths along with your personality and attributes, unique gifts, and passions.

YOUR ACCOMPLISHMENTS make you attractive to an employer or client and talking about them helps people see how you fit into the team and the organization. What are your high-impact accomplishments? What are you most proud of?

YOUR SPECIALTY is your niche. Be sure to list all your professional titles, credentials, certifications, publications, and awards.

PERSONALITY is the way you convey your talents, specialties, and accomplishments to others. You have inherited a host of personality traits that are influenced by your environment, your upbringing, and your efforts. One of our colleagues is an extrovert and her warmth is a huge part of her reputation and her personality. It's a key ingredient to her effectiveness.

TALENTS AND GIFTS Identify unique abilities—your differentiators. Think about the compliments you have received from friends and co-workers. What do you enjoy doing? For example, maybe you have a gift for managing projects or seeing possibilities. Perhaps you have a talent for calming tense situations or solving sticky problems.

YOUR PASSIONS describe your personality when you're at your best. What activities boost your energy and spark your drive? In what environments do you feel engaged, enthusiastic, and confident?

Carly, a senior manager in one of our workshops, was starting a new role with a new team. She wanted to get an early good start and was eager to get her story together. She told us that making sense of her past was confusing. How could she talk about her history and keep it relevant to the work ahead? How could she be brief and present herself as a strong leader? What were the most important things the team really needed to know about her? Who should she connect with and what should she share with them?

She completed an exercise called the Message Triangle that helped her identify accomplishments, talents, specialty/niche, and passions. Then Carly added real examples and stories (see figure 6 on the next page). Laying them out in the message triangle

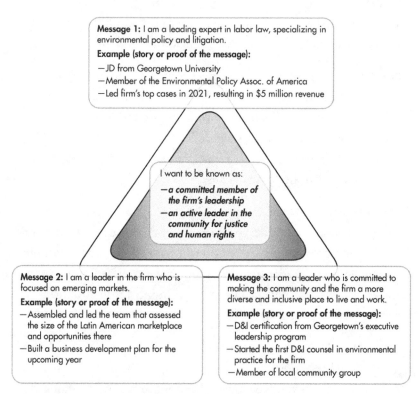

Figure 6. A Message Triangle example

helped her visualize her story. This exercise, based on public relations concepts, marries key accomplishments with examples to drive home an intentional message. This works for organizations, causes, and brands, and it will work for individuals as well. See Carly's example above. Then try it for yourself.

Using the Three D's: Define, Design, and Demonstrate

Now that you have completed the Message Triangle, this exercise, based on three D words, will help you further craft your message.

DEFINE Review previous feedback or performance reviews. Have a third party conduct interviews for feedback on your behalf. This will help you see whether or not others' experience with you and perception of you fits with how you see yourself and your career goals. Ask trusted people, "What comes to mind when people hear my name?" or "What do you think I'm known for around here?" "What do people say about me when I'm not in the room?" Consider what accomplishments you want to be known for. How would you describe your personality when you're at your best?

DESIGN With research in hand, it's time to design. Make a list of words and phrases that consistently appear in the feedback you've gathered. Reflect on what you want to be known for. Are there specialties or niches you can or want to stake a claim to? Are there gaps between what people see and what you want them to see? How can you fill them? What are four key messages you want others to take away after they've spent time with you?

DEMONSTRATE Once you have clarity about what your brand is or should be, it's time for action. This step fleshes out the details of your work in a compelling way so you can clearly convey it to others. Make a list of the opportunities that allow you to talk about and continually build on your reputationality.

In our workshops, we get women thinking about the power of a strong brand by asking them to stand up, close their eyes, and imagine shopping for a pair of shoes. We suggest that they decide exactly what pair of shoes they're going to buy and sit down when they've made that decision. Within five seconds, all the women are seated. It never fails to be that quick. When we ask them what brand they chose and why, we get a wide range of responses. They choose Cole Haan for comfort, Jimmy Choo for style, Nike for performance. They are keenly aware of the attributes that a brand offers in the context of their needs and criteria. This is the point. How quickly does a name come to mind when a need is presented?

That is how quickly choices can be made in the workplace. When a need or an opportunity arises, a specific person often comes to mind. That is the power of reputation capital, an asset that is more likely to put you on the radar when choices are being made.

Find Your Three Words

In workshops, we show slides with photos of famous people. We ask participants to say who the person is and describe them in two or three words. Here are examples of the responses we get:

Oprah Winfrey: Brilliant, Brave, Real

Lady Gaga: Talented, Outlandish, Versatile

Serena Williams: Winner, Badass, Intense

Then we ask them to imagine their own faces on that screen. What words would their colleagues and constituents use to describe them? More important, what words would they *want* their colleagues to use? A powerful message will clearly communicate values, skills, talents, achievements, focus, and personality. All of those things are differentiators.

Write Your Introduction

Another way we get women thinking about reputationality is by asking them to do a two-minute introduction. Think of it as a way to give people a sense of who you are and what you've accomplished.

In one session we did, Beatriz, an engineer in her late 30s, talked to a workshop group about her impressive academic pedigree, how she had landed her job, a few elements of her job description, and how long she'd been with her company. After, when we asked questions, we discovered that Beatriz was one of a handful of people in the country who had expertise in a very narrow area of her field. It was an impressive specialty, but she didn't mention it until we pressed her.

We work with a lot of women who "bury the lead" in this way. We've had women talk about various aspects of their career and forget to mention that they have a law degree or a PhD or a specialty certification or that they have won a prestigious award. People shouldn't have to become investigative reporters to find out the best and truest parts of your story. Resist the temptation to downplay your achievements or gloss over your accomplishments because you think it shows a lack of humility.

Start an Accomplishment Log

One great way to pay attention to reputationality is by maintaining an accomplishment log on paper or on your computer or both. The most important thing is not where you keep it, it's that you're constantly attending to it, just as you would water a garden so the plants will thrive.

When you hit a big milestone on a project, earn a credential, publish an article, organize a forum or peer group, serve on a committee, or speak at a conference, those achievements go into your file. Copy and file every memo of praise from colleagues, managers, or customers. Any time you feel proud of an achievement, such as saving the company money or coming up with a creative solution to a sticky problem, make note of the details. Jot down quantitative or anecdotal information that can add richness to your stories and strengthen your message.

Spend time on your accomplishment log consistently, once a week or once a month. This will keep your reputationality top of mind, and as a bonus, it will be a great resource for your annual performance evaluation. Consistently reflect on the ways you want to package yourself and plan a strategy for communicating your personal brand.

STEP 1: Think about and record your key accomplishments. Put time in your calendar once or twice a month to record your accomplishments. Consider using a journal.

STEP 2: Find a time interval that is right for you to come back and reflect on the accomplishments you have logged. It could be every two weeks or every few months. For projects or significant contributions at work or in the community, consider and respond to the following questions:

> What challenges did I face?
>
> What was innovative about the way I approached the situation?
>
> What were the unusual solutions created or unexpected problems I helped solve?
>
> What actions did I take?
>
> What were the results?
>
> What was my impact on key constituencies?

Take time to describe the results in visual and vivid ways and create distinctions using relevant data.

STEP 3: Step back and look for patterns and tie them back to the themes of your brand. A clear understanding of yourself creates expectations. It clearly communicates values, skills, talents, personality, and focus. It powerfully and succinctly lets others know what you do and what differentiates you from your peers.

Know your personality. Highly effective leaders never stop learning who they are, the advantages of their personality, and how their personality makes them different. One woman we coached, the chief strategy officer at her company, was an introverted leader. Feedback consistently showed she was known for being contemplative, thoughtful, questioning, and deliberate. Not only was this part of her personality, it was the cornerstone of her strong brand. The CEO considered her his top replacement. The combination of strong skills and credentials and her personality attributes was powerful. It opened doors for her.

Spotlight your reputationality. Answer questions, or start conversations, with phrases such as:

> "I had a wonderful opportunity to do something I love with some great colleagues who share my passion."

> "I am so excited that I found a creative way to save the company money."

> "I'm challenged by resources for the project I'm leading, but I found a solution by . . ."

Note the intentional use of the pronoun "I." Women often use "we," and sometimes they should. But remember that illuminating your reputationality is all about you. Look for scenarios, audiences, and individual conversations in which you can share your stories over a cup of coffee with a colleague or manager, in the introductions at a meeting, or during a networking happy hour. Have three or four talking points or stories ready that highlight the aspects of your work that reinforce your brand.

THE STORIES THAT HOLD US BACK

Women tend to think about reputationality in terms of being known for the work they do. That's part of it, sure, but we see it as so much more. Reputationality is a way to powerfully leverage the totality of your accomplishments, enhance your reputation, and gain influence.

Limiting mindsets can derail such efforts:

> "Everyone should know what I'm doing. Why do I need to talk about it?"

"I'm not going to brag about my work."

"I'm a team player. I dislike trying to take credit for successful projects."

"If I do my job well, I'll get noticed."

"I am who I am and I'm not going to fake it or change or try to be someone I'm not."

"I'm not political, so I don't want to go around promoting myself."

"My work is visible to all, and that should speak for itself."

"Talking about my accomplishments is self-serving and distasteful."

When we're able to persuade women of the value of reputationality, their next statement is often, "Who has the time for that?" Such thinking is not conducive to cogent career building.

Alicia, who was in her mid-40s, was an up-and-coming leader in an engineering company where she had worked for more than fifteen years. Her career seemed to be on a beautiful upward trajectory. She worked hard, she had developed solid client relationships, and she maintained respectable billings.

Among her passions was mentoring young talent. Alicia loved helping advance women and knew that this was becoming an important initiative for her company. To that end, she created forums where women could join peer groups and organized a quarterly breakfast so women in the practice could get to know each other and network.

When she learned of a promotion opportunity that would enable her to lead an industry segment in which she had expertise, Alicia figured her hard work would pay off, particularly her efforts that dovetailed with the firm's goals of growing the practice and attracting diverse talent. In addition, she had good relationships with most of the executive team. Alicia felt confident as she applied for the promotion.

The role did, in fact, go to a woman, but it wasn't Alicia. The company made an external hire, a woman who was well known for her connections in the industry segment and for her community-based work to support professional women. The firm asked the new hire to spearhead the firm's effort to attract, retain, and advance women.

Alicia felt doubly devastated. As she processed her disappointment, she was determined to figure out why she hadn't landed the job. As she asked for and received feedback from people she trusted, she discovered that her reputation was solid. People saw her as someone who was adept at managing key clients and as a strong biller. But here was the kicker: while most people were familiar with the women's groups she had created and fostered, she had failed to talk explicitly and strategically with others about the changes, value, and benefits her extracurricular work had generated for the firm. She hadn't told her story with passion. She had figured that her work would speak for itself. After all, she had organized the forums, she was always at the events, and she made a point of greeting people and making introductions. But no one had identified Alicia as the one who was driving those efforts. Assumptions that her work spoke for itself meant that she had inadvertently limited the power and impact of her efforts.

Alicia went to work on being more deliberate about her reputationality. She focused on efforts to promote herself and her good work. Working with her coaches and with feedback from trusted colleagues, she crafted key messages that would showcase her work in an authentic way without veering into boasting. She included statements that reflected her aspirational interests as well as her accomplishments in helping women advance in the workplace. She made sure leadership saw her strategic work. Eighteen months later, she landed a new leadership role.

THE POWER OF REFRAMING: NEW STORY

So many women value the ability to be genuine in their approaches. How they do what they do is almost inseparable from the end result they target. This is why the authentic side of who they are— the style, approach, and perspective they bring from experience— is an important part of the reputationality equation.

Marina, an experienced engineer, led a team that was responsible for building out the highways for a large municipality in California. She recognized that several key leaders needed to know her and her work better. However, after the pandemic began in 2020, opportunities to see those leaders face to face vanished. She hesitated to act because the voice in her head told her that supervisors and relevant colleagues "should already know this about me. I've been here a long enough time."

With coaching sessions, she decided to silence that voice and experiment with other approaches. The work Marina did brought value to the organization and to the city. It was time for her to start sharing milestones from a position of strength.

After a client sent an email complimenting her and the team for their good work, she shared it with a few team members and decided to keep the promotional momentum going. Marina forwarded the complimentary note to three leaders with a message that read:

"Bob, Sara and Gil: I have been leading a team of engineers this past year on a transportation project for the city. Transportation planning for municipalities is my primary area of focus, and I look forward to sharing more about this work with you soon. Meanwhile, I thought you might appreciate the note below from the client. They are extremely pleased with the completion of Phase One, which is a $2 million investment. Of course, I also shared this email with my team, a talented group of engineers that I assembled for this work. Let me know if you have questions. As the project lead, I wanted to make sure you knew about this project and the value it's bringing to the firm!"

After she hit the send button, Marina sat back with some relief and a little pride. She had finally said what she might not have been able to say while standing in a coffee line with Bob, Sara, or Gil. Her key talking points: I have expertise. I have a great client. I am managing a multimillion-dollar project. I assemble great teams. The clients are happy with me and my team's work.

She decided this was a much more useful brand for her. Her note felt authentic and the tone was enthusiastic and accurate—not bragging, just a direct statement of facts. Nor had she taken all the credit. Marina felt confident and a great satisfaction at having communicated a specific accomplishment and the value of her work.

Even more gratifying? The leaders' response to Marina's email. Bob wrote an email with a huge "THANK YOU" in the subject line and asked to set up a call to learn more about the project and her work. Sara also sent a thank-you, adding, "I'm so glad you sent this. I have a call with Tim from the city next week, and I bet he's going to talk about the project. Now I know where we are with it!" Gil, who didn't yet know her, also expressed gratitude. He wrote that he was delighted to finally have an introduction and looked forward to working with her. Marina filed all these notes in a newly created "Accomplishments Log," which she intends to keep up to date.

A simple act. A prepared and genuine message. The right audience. A perfect blend of reputation and personality coming together to own the work. This is reputationality.

Get a clear understanding of who you are, what you care about, and how you do what you do.

Tell people what you do well and what you want to do. This can open more opportunities to do the work you aspire to.

Define your brand to minimize the risk that others will define it for you in a way you don't prefer.

Share your wins and opportunities. People you work for and with are busy. They can't possibly know everything they should about what you're doing and the value you bring.

In addition to what you are doing, you are continually becoming. Managing this process with purpose gives a lift to your work, your energy, and your aspirations. During the early years of Jeanne's career, she focused on the work itself, her technical expertise, and making her mark in the profession. Because she was in a male-dominated technology field, Jeanne believed she needed to behave in ways that were similar to the way her male colleagues behaved. The work environment accentuated her more aggressive tendencies, but she didn't believe that adequately represented who she really was.

Jeanne told us that she finally put reputation and personality together while working with a coach. It changed everything.

Understanding the reputationality she wanted to project enabled her to communicate more clearly who she was as a person and what she had accomplished in her career and leverage her style. As a woman leader, she felt she could be her authentic self and let go of the expectations she had associated with the male-oriented culture. She told us that she wishes she had realized this thirty years ago.

When you clarify your reputationality, your colleagues, clients, and others will understand your best and highest value better and know how to influence people on your behalf. If you and others don't know your story, you're far less likely to be a contender when coveted projects, promotions, and assignments appear, as Alicia and Colleen found out the hard way.

Lida Citroën, a branding expert and the author of *Control the Narrative*, states it well: "Everyone has a brand, by design or by default."[5] We strongly encourage you to design your brand and constantly think about the most effective ways to market yourself.

COACH ON YOUR SHOULDER
Advice for Steering Clear of the Blind Spot

BUILD BUZZ In the interviews we conduct to get feedback for women we coach, one of our questions is, "What's the buzz about her?" Drawing on the examples and stories in your message triangle, use informal conversations in the hallways, the cafeteria, over coffee, and in the bathroom to reinforce your reputationality. Give people something to think about, talk about, or share with others. These chats are designed to shine a light on the most important aspects of you as defined by you.

KNOW YOUR AUDIENCE Make a list of people who need to know you—stakeholders, decision-makers, board members, influencers, or others. This list doesn't have to be long, just focused. Keep it updated with a few details about when you last spoke with them. Did you commit to follow up? When will you reach out to them again? Take time to prepare and understand what is relevant to them.

LEVERAGE YOUR PERSONALITY AS PART OF YOUR REPUTATION One of our colleagues is a strong business leader who has had to make hard decisions about people and processes. She also is exceptionally kind and has often been told she needed to be more hard nosed. But years ago, she made an intentional decision to let her kindness be a big part of her decision-making process and communication style, especially when it came to messages that might be hard for people to hear. She practiced the ability to allow kindness to come through even when the situation demanded difficult decisions. This gave her reputationality a distinct flavor and differentiated her from other leaders. What part of your personality can be part of your reputation?

ALIGN YOUR ONLINE REPUTATIONALITY A CareerBuilder survey conducted in 2018 showed that 70 percent of employers use social media to screen potential employees and 43 percent use it to check on current employees.[6] Internal promotions can hang on an employee's reputation. Do a focused inventory on all of your media (both social accounts and the more professionally focused ones such as LinkedIn). Are your messages aligned with your intention? Review your résumé and write a short bio that summarizes the messages you want to broadcast. In our coaching, women tend to see this work as "dreaded housekeeping." Do a mental reframing of this task. Time spent on reputationality and your messages is an investment in your career.

USE "I" VERSUS "WE" It is great to give credit to the team, but it is critical to help others understand your specific role in what got accomplished. Practice making the distinction. "I assembled the team for this project and set the direction for the work." Step into the spotlight. It's a gift when you help people understand who you are, what you can do, and what you want to do.

PREPARE TO REINVENT The strategic goals of markets, companies, and industries constantly evolve. So should your credentials, style, and aspirations. Monitor trends and prepare to shift when the opportunities arise so your reputationality stays fresh and relevant. After the 2008 economic crash, one client repurposed her capabilities in banking technology to become a leading consultant in the asset management industry. Consistent, intentional work on reputationality enables you to reframe, reinvent, repurpose, and reengage. Once you have reinvented yourself, repackage your messages and select the audiences that need to know what you're doing.

You are known for something. Figure out what it is and whether it matches what you want. Use these strategies to keep your reputationality sharp, relevant, and intentional. As one of our colleagues used to say, "Go get famous for something!" Grab your broom, light the fire, and start waving.

SUMMARY:
What We Want You to Know

- Reputationality merges the work you do with the person you are.
- Building your reputationality is essential. If you don't do it, people may define it for you in a way you don't prefer.
- It's not enough to know your reputationality. Develop effective communication strategies that help you highlight your accomplishments and advertise your achievements.
- Find opportunities to share with others what you've accomplished, what excites you, and what your career goals are.
- Creating reputationality helps you get the attention of decision-makers and influencers.

CHAPTER FOUR

Operating on Autopilot

Install a Career GPS

Everything in my environment is offering me feedback,
if I would only listen.

—SHARON WEIL, AUTHOR AND FILMMAKER

Without good, real-time guidance, finding your way takes a lot more effort than it needs to. And while it's true that not all who wander are lost, wandering is an inefficient way to get there for those who have a destination in mind.

Among the advantages of today's reliable GPS systems are immediate alerts that tell you when you're headed in the wrong direction, when there is congestion ahead, or when a traffic accident is creating dangerous conditions. You get real-time information about obstacles up ahead so you can adjust in a way that gets you where you want to be more quickly. If the train conductor in our story of Peggy and her broom on fire had been guided by a good GPS system, he would have known what was around the bend and Peggy's heroic efforts would have been unnecessary.

It's no different when you're navigating a career. We talked in chapter 1 about the importance of a vision and strategy to establish the destination you desire. But to get there, you need continual, real-time guidance to minimize the risk of taking an inefficient route or getting lost along the way. You need to develop a system that will suggest alternate routes or suggest a U-turn if you're headed in the wrong direction. You need access to right-now information to guide your career journey.

Without such a system, you will be proceeding without reliable information about progress and how you are perceived by others—a serious career disadvantage. That's why we continually beat the drum about proactively seeking feedback, advice, and coaching that can help you guide and occasionally correct your course. A process and a supportive system augment your internal guidance and point to different paths or directions when it becomes necessary.

Lydia, a senior manager at a manufacturing company, was slightly dumbfounded and frustrated as Brenda delivered a feedback report. The report was based on interviews and survey questions answered by Lydia's co-workers, managers, colleagues, and peers. Throughout their coaching sessions, she'd told Brenda that she was determined to continue her ascent on the management track. Her goal was necessary, she said with a laugh, because "I have three kids to get through college. Moving up that ladder is very important!"

Lydia had a big personality. She was personable and fun loving. The feedback about her was generally very good. Her team members and others respected her and saw her as competent, hardworking, and easy to work with. What was the issue? A consistent theme in the data Brenda had gathered showed that she wasn't perceived as a "tough enough" leader for the next level of management. Her colleagues' perception was that she had a hard time delivering difficult feedback and making tough calls.

At first, Lydia wasn't having it. "What?" she said, her tone disbelieving and defensive. "That's not true. I am tough!" She pointed out that she had recently reorganized her team and had made hard decisions to move people out who weren't performing. "I can be tough when I need to be—in fact, I just put one of my direct reports on a performance improvement plan!"

The company's culture called for senior leaders to be strong, firm, and committed to achieving the goals of the company. Being "tough" was a crucial characteristic for those who wanted to continue up the management ladder. To be promoted, Lydia needed to be perceived as someone who set high expectations, drove performance, and achieved results that strengthened the business.

While she saw herself as having those characteristics, it was clear from the feedback report that others did not. That gap created a dilemma. Although Lydia disagreed with the perception, Brenda pointed out that others' perceptions constitute their reality. Lydia was being shown a reality she needed to address.

THE BLIND SPOT: NAVIGATING YOUR CAREER WITHOUT GOOD GUIDANCE

Receiving good feedback, digesting it, and integrating it in a way that serves your career trajectory is one of the most neglected aspects of successful career management. This is a glaring blind spot because it prevents women from making career course corrections before it's too late.

The lack of consistent feedback is problematic. Most employees get feedback only during an annual performance review. Too often we hear from the women we coach that they don't know where they stand in their career or what people think of them.

Feedback is trickier for women than it is for men. Women are more likely to get feedback that is less actionable and less effective than that given to men. Research shows that "developmental feedback for female employees tends to focus on delivery rather than vision, coping with politics rather than leveraging politics, and collaboration rather than assertiveness. It also tends to present a lack of confidence as a fundamental shortcoming rather than a specific skill that can be developed."[1]

Elena Doldor, Madeleine Wyatt, and Jo Silvester, experts in leadership and diversity in organizations, argue that the goal isn't to treat women more like men but rather to encourage leadership characteristics and practices that incorporate the best of what are seen as traditionally feminine and masculine traits. They offer advice for ways that managers can give more impactful feedback and suggest ways women can elicit feedback that points to actions they can take.[2] For example, you could ask questions or make statements such as:

> "You know my leadership style, so how would you advise me to navigate this challenging project I'm leading?"
>
> "I would appreciate your insights on how to manage the stakeholders on the new rollout."
>
> "Let me tell you about my leadership aspirations, and I'd love your feedback on who or what might enable me to achieve them."

The solution to lack of good feedback, the experts suggest, is for you to create conscious feedback processes that help guide you toward career goals and enhance others' perceptions of you as someone who is serious about the business.

These circumstances are among the reasons we do extensive 360-degree interviews for women we work with. We know from research and long experience that they often don't have good sources of feedback. In thousands of assessments we have done, we've learned that everyone has blind spots. They are a fact of life. Feedback brings others' perceptions into the light of day so the women we coach have the power to deal with them.

Through proactively cultivating feedback and advice from others, you can get a better sense of how you're perceived and where you might find personal growth opportunities. This is a personalized career GPS, if you will. Author and teacher Sylvia Boorstein talks about the gentle direction her GPS device gives her when she veers off track. "If I make a mistake, it says, 'recalculating,'" Boorstein said, which alerts her to changes she needs to make.[3] This is what real-time feedback does for you in the professional environment.

We have watched this blind spot sidetrack, stall, or derail women's careers. Knowledge about how others see you is another way to become powerful. If you're willing to reflect on and integrate the information and advice you get, the "recalculation" will be invaluable in guiding you to a successful career. Developing and maintaining a career GPS can quickly put you on a more productive path.

PERILS OF THE BLIND SPOT

When you feel lost or unsure about how to get where you want to go, what is the logical thing to do? It would make sense to ask for directions from someone who knows the terrain and is familiar with the streetscape. People with experience and expertise may even be able to help you find a few shortcuts.

The danger of *not* doing this is real. While you may eventually arrive where you want to be, you will have wasted a lot of time and energy. It's like being in a car stuck in sand—the wheels are spinning and you're not getting anywhere. In the worst-case scenario, you might find yourself so lost that you drive off a career cliff. This happened to two female executives at a major investment banking firm in New York.

When two women made it to the top of a large, prestigious investment banking firm that had historically been dominated by men, it was a groundbreaking, hope-inspiring moment. Both women had successfully worked up through the company's ranks over many years, and their promotions were hailed as a sea change in the company's culture. But after about a year, both women left the company. One of the senior executives at the firm knew that these women had always been goal driven and successful, and he recognized that firing them was problematic. What had happened? He hired Kathryn to conduct an analysis.

For several weeks, Kathryn interviewed people in the firm to gather information about why these highly competent, hardworking women had not succeeded in an arena where they had typically flourished. The major themes she heard were that the women were really great. Everyone had been excited and expectant. But several of those interviewed said that the women had begun to make mistakes or "mess up." One of the women, several colleagues said, had created a new financial product that had failed spectacularly, creating a big financial hit for the firm.

Unfortunately, Kathryn didn't have access to the two women, so she couldn't get their perspective of the situation or learn about what circumstances might have been outside their control. But among the things she wanted to discover was how she could help the company make changes so that other women's careers wouldn't get derailed. She also wanted to discover what other women could learn from the situation that might benefit their career navigation.

She asked the women's male colleagues: "If you saw them making mistakes, why didn't you tell them? Why didn't you help?" The answers, which fell into four general categories, were illuminating.

The first had to do with professional competence. Because the women had reached such a high level, their colleagues felt they should know what they were doing. As senior leaders, they were supposed to have answers and resources to create their own success. At that career level, colleagues said, they shouldn't have needed hand-holding and feedback to prevent them from making mistakes.

Others said they didn't know the women well, so they felt uncomfortable about giving them advice. Male colleagues also said that they worried that offering unsolicited feedback might upset the women. When Kathryn pressed them about what "upset" looked like, it often came down to "I was afraid she would get emotional." Some mentioned the fear of an angry display or tears.

Several said that offering the women feedback might be seen as inappropriate and worried they'd land in trouble with human resources. And a fourth theme boiled down to women being high maintenance when they get feedback. They said things such as: "When you give women feedback, they start asking a bunch of questions." Kathryn recognized herself in the last comment. During her corporate career, she typically asked a lot of questions in the wake of feedback but had never considered that it would be perceived as a negative quality.

As Kathryn waited in the hallway just before delivering her report to the executives who had hired her, she watched two male employees chatting as they walked down the hall together, their eyes glued to their cell phones. Apparently, they had just come from a presentation, and one of them said to the other, "The way you did that close didn't work. You really need to change it." And without looking up from his phone or hesitating, his colleague replied, "Yep, you're right. Gonna work on that."

It struck Kathryn as a micro-lesson about the different ways men and women typically deliver and receive feedback. When she asked male colleagues about this interaction she'd witnessed, they confirmed that this was typical. The men told her that feedback should be quick, unemotional, and just in time. They talked about how such mini-corrections had benefited their careers. They compared it to athletes who get immediate coaching to improve performance in real time.

After Kathryn delivered her feedback report to the company's senior executives, they expressed dismay and embarrassment. They vowed to make changes. And among the lessons Kathryn took back to her female clients was that high-level competence and achieving senior leadership isn't necessarily enough. While Kathryn couldn't be sure whether the two female executives had asked for feedback, it was clear that their male colleagues hadn't been proactive about offering it. She could definitely see how developing a system to get real-time information would give women a better shot at course corrections before careers were endangered.

The world needs more women leaders. We see too many women who veer off course, and we don't want that for you. The act of cultivating feedback is a high-level skill. We consider it crucial to a successful career. Making this a strong practice will help you make progress more quickly than just about any other thing you can do. Set it up by deciding who you will ask, how often you will ask, and what specific information and feedback you want from peers and colleagues.

COACH ON YOUR SHOULDER
Questions to Help You Reflect on Where You Are

- How and when do you reflect on your performance?
- Do you avoid asking for feedback, and if so, why?
- How well do you read others' reactions to you and your ideas?
- Who are the people you can turn to for feedback and advice?
- What steps can you take to influence others' perceptions of you?
- What actions will help you become a continuous personal learner?

STRATEGIES

In Boorstein's podcast interview, she talked about the futility of getting angry or defensive when the GPS tells her it's recalculating. "You could get mad. You could go home. You could tell a few people you can't believe what this person said," Boorstein said. "Indignation is tremendously seductive." However, if you're on the wrong road, the wiser choice is to recognize the misdirection and be grateful for the warning: "Wait a minute. This way won't get me where I want to go." Boorstein also notes that feedback is *information* rather than a value judgment: "No matter how many times I don't make that turn, [the GPS] will continue to say, 'Recalculating.' The tone of voice will stay the same."[4]

Mikaela, for example, received direct feedback that she wasn't managing her managers and those in her upward chain of command well and was told that the relationship she had with her supervisor was negatively affecting the team. Her response? "Thank you for letting me know that. I will work on it." Her non-defensive acceptance of the feedback was important and so was her follow-through. She took actions that were directly tied to the ways she worked with her boss and then reported back. Reporting back not only reinforced her new behaviors, it also communicated to her team, "I heard you. Here is what I'm actively doing to change this. Please give me feedback if you see me doing things that aren't helpful in achieving our goals." After a few months, she received fresh feedback. "You've done it. You've changed the relationship and served the business." It's all about setting up an understanding of what you specifically want from others so they can help you achieve a goal.

In qualitative research our company did in 2021, we interviewed thirty-seven women who had reached senior executive leadership positions. The core competencies that were strongly present in 100 percent of the women, regardless of their other competencies or career paths, were tenacity, agility, and continuous learning.

When you actively ask for feedback and graciously thank people for their help, you are signaling that you're interested in continuous learning. In their book *The Career Architect Development Planner*, Robert Eichinger and Michael Lombardo describe learning agility as a "silver bullet."[5] Cynthia, a client who managed a rapid ascent in her career, told us that the main reason she kept getting promoted was that she had a reputation for curiosity and a love of learning. She was known for being receptive to feedback. Her colleagues and supervisors saw her openness as a key strength.

Asking for help also is a way of enrolling someone on your team. You're enlisting them in your career. Never underestimate the importance of influencing other people to see you in the way you want to be seen. While feedback doesn't necessarily *require* you to change, it offers valuable data about the reasons you might want to change based on how others see you. Women often struggle with changes that they believe compromise their values or integrity. We say that you always get to choose what to incorporate and whether to change at all. People's perceptions are their reality and arguing with others' reality is rarely useful. If you're getting similar feedback from multiple people, doesn't that deserve examination? You're far better off considering and possibly embracing feedback so you can actively find ways to alter perceptions. We use the graphic shown in figure 7 with clients to illuminate the way a perception cycle can work:

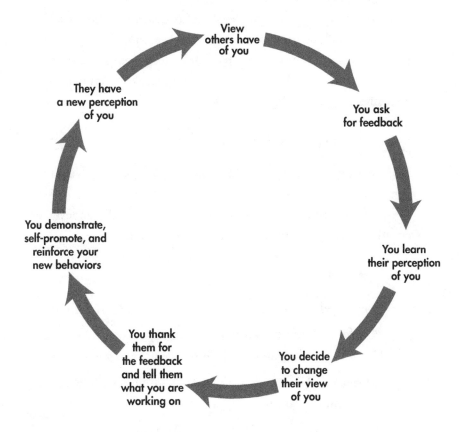

Figure 7. The perception cycle

Everything begins with self-awareness, a skill set we encourage you to develop continuously (see chapter 2). Leaders who are self-aware are typically more effective, in part because self-awareness signals good emotional intelligence. Becoming aware of your own emotional reactions can help you manage others. If you can see that people aren't reacting positively to an idea you're pitching in a meeting, notice what signals they're sending. Does their tone of voice change, their body language, their facial expressions? Do they talk slower or faster?

If you're trying to persuade others or learn something about yourself, pay close attention to how they react to what you're saying. This is another way to get feedback. Resistance is a comment on your communication and could signal that you need to change your message or the way you deliver it.

STORIES THAT HOLD US BACK

Even with great strategies and good coaching, we've found that competent women can get tripped up by their limiting beliefs. We often hear statements like the ones below, and the underlying emotions that fuel them come up time and again:

"It often ends up hurting my feelings when I get feedback, so I don't ask."

"I can't help what other people think of me. I am tired of hearing about others' feelings."

"I don't know how to not take it personally, so I get defensive."

"What I'm doing now works for me. I'm good at my job, so why would I want to change?"

"No one has said anything, so I must be doing OK."

"I am who I am. Examining my assumptions won't change me."

"Asking for feedback or information is too time consuming."

"If I ask for feedback or advice, people will think I don't know what I am doing."

The underlying cause of limiting beliefs is often fear. Hearing that you need to change might wound your ego or hurt your feelings. You might worry that people will see you as incompetent, unskilled, or lacking in knowledge. Are you afraid that people see you as "less than" if you don't have it all figured out? Will it hurt your chances in the future?

Let's try looking at it in a different way. What if you could view feedback as a gift? Instead of hearing that you're "less than," you could hear that someone cares enough about you and your success to give you useful information, even if it's hard to hear. They're sharing with you the story in *their* head, and you can't just wave a magic wand to change the story. What is the downside to seriously considering what about their story might have relevant, helpful information?

Sometimes when women get feedback they aren't ready to hear, they will say something like, "What is the point of taking it seriously? I'm not going to change." But if someone holds up a mirror, they're just asking you to see what they see, not necessarily telling you they don't like the person who is reflected there. Examining the reflection might spark insight, and again, you always have the power to choose whether to change.

Few things are more advantageous for women than knowing their strengths and where they stand. This will minimize derailers and accentuate powerful traits. Yet no state is static. Life is constantly shifting. If women want to keep themselves and their goals on track, cultivating, listening to, and integrating relevant feedback will give them a valuable assist. If knowledge is power, self-knowledge is exponential power.

THE POWER OF REFRAMING: NEW STORY

After Lydia, the client mentioned at the beginning of this chapter, reflected on the findings in her assessment, she and Brenda put together a plan. Although Lydia still saw herself as a disciplined manager who knew when to be tough, one of her primary goals was to change her co-workers' perceptions that she wasn't. Her plan was to use conversation and self-promotion to influence the way people saw her.

During meetings, Lydia began discussing some of the tough decisions she had to make and how she was going to make them and then reporting back to her team on what had happened. She talked transparently about the need to give people difficult feedback and talked about the specific ways she delivered it. She followed up with her team, offering details about challenging situations and conversations and how she'd managed them. Lydia consistently integrated terms like "the necessity for excellence" and talked firmly and frequently about the actions she was taking to enhance her team's performance and drive good results.

In addition, Lydia recruited a few trusted peers to give her feedback on how she was doing. She explained what she hoped to accomplish and asked them to alert her if they saw her taking actions that didn't get her closer to the goal. One peer mentioned that one of Lydia's direct reports had behaviors that were interfering with productivity and that other people thought that Lydia was blind to these behaviors. She thanked her colleague for their honesty and outlined what she intended to do about the situation. After she took action, she reported back to her colleague what steps had been taken to get her employee back on track.

Her tactics paid off. When Brenda did a follow-up assessment after six months, the comments about Lydia's lack of toughness had disappeared. When Brenda pressed people about that specific characteristic, she got a collective shrug. No one saw it as an issue.

Lydia continued to assert to Brenda that her behavior hadn't changed much. She felt certain that the feedback had changed because she had actively and frequently talked about her ability to be tough and used detailed examples to back up her assertions. Lydia was gratified that she had successfully changed a perception that could have been an obstacle to her career goals.

Feedback Is Your Friend

We've jokingly talked about creating T-shirts with these words boldly emblazoned on the front as a gift for all our clients. If you can learn to see it as a kind offer of help, as a gift, it will help you dismantle the defensiveness or anger that feedback sometimes invokes. And if defensiveness is your instinctive reaction, that just makes you human. Ideally, you'll find a way to manage your ego in a way that allows you to move past it so you can more objectively ponder the information you've been given and mine it for what could be valuable.

Feed Forward

Often when people hear the word "feedback," there is a figurative eye roll. We ask the women we coach to think about it differently. Feedback is the process of learning new information and discovering different ways to operate in the future. One banker we worked with used to say he loved customer comments because they told him what he needed to know about how to improve. In our programs, we ask peers to help each other and frame the focus as "What would you do differently next time to make it better?" This helps the recipient consider how to think forward instead of ruminating or feeling bad about behavior or performance.

Find a Way to Get Coached

As with any discipline that requires practice, coaching can help you improve. Leadership is a challenging skill that requires practice to get better. Getting guidance from a coach can help improve your performance more quickly. If you don't have the resources to hire a coach, create your own. Find people who are willing to be direct and honest with you about your performance and offer to do the same for them.

Consider "After-Action Reviews"

An after-action review is a post-event analysis to understand what went as expected, what didn't go as planned, and how to improve results. This strategy originated with the U.S. Army in the 1970s.[6] If you know you're going to be directing a project, delivering a presentation, chairing a committee, or hosting a town hall, be prepared to have a debriefing with people who were involved. Sometimes people, wanting to be kind and supportive, will say things such as, "You did a great job!" One of our clients, Mercedes, wants more. She responds, "That doesn't really help me." Even though she might feel good about how a presentation went, she will ask people to give her specific ways to improve. "If you were me," she asks, "what is one thing you would change to make the presentation better?" You can also reflect and journal later. One woman we know created a spreadsheet to help her track what she did, the feedback she received, and what she learned from that information.

Hearing feedback with neutrality can be a potent skill and will help you understand the difference between feedback and criticism. Take a page from actors and athletes. The best ones understand that feedback is performance enhancing. They consistently get and even ask for in-the-moment direction from their coaches, teammates, and other cast members that will help them do their jobs better. They know they can't afford to wait until after the game is over or the show has closed to make improvements.

COACH ON YOUR SHOULDER
Tips for Steering Clear of the Blind Spot

ASK FOR ADVICE Often people think of feedback as something negative, dark, and potentially hurtful. If asking for feedback sounds too hard, ask for *advice* instead. Asking "Can you advise me about a challenge I'm facing?" could ease some of the tension. Explain the specifics of a dilemma or problem or your concerns about how people perceive you and ask, "How might you handle this?" Feedback is information, and information is power. You don't necessarily have to act on it, but you do need to understand other people's perceptions.

ALL FEEDBACK IS NOT CREATED EQUALLY Many people can give you feedback, but some are more important to hear from than others. Be brave. Ask for feedback from those who might not be your biggest supporters or who have not known you long but could have an interesting perspective on you. Solicit feedback from people who might have more influence over your career than others.

UNDERSTAND THE BUSINESS A career consists of more than just "getting your work done." It includes learning the specifics of running the business and making a profit. This is often referred to as learning the "business of the business." How does what you do connect to business results? What is your company's core mission and its business objectives? What are the key measures? Knowing the company's goals and strategies can help you make decisions that contribute to business success and is a visible demonstration that you're committed to understanding the big picture. A consistent theme in feedback assessments we do for women is, "She needs to learn more about how the business operates and how we make money."

ALLOW TIME FOR REFLECTION When you ask for feedback or advice, let people know ahead of time so they have time to think about what they want to say. You're likely to get better, more thoughtful feedback if people have time to reflect and don't feel like they've been put on the spot. Allocate time for reflection in your daily or weekly routine. If you're squeezed for time, maybe you can use your commute time. Or you could block out a couple of hours on your calendar for the specific task of focusing on what kind of feedback you've received or areas where you'd benefit from more data on how you're doing. Pay attention to the voices in your head and the stories you're telling yourself.

LOOK FOR A COACHING BUDDY A mutually beneficial coaching relationship can do wonders for self-improvement and strengthening performance. For example, if you want to sharpen your ability to speak up in meetings or ask insightful, relevant questions, let your buddy know you need advice and feedback after each meeting and make a pact to do the same for them. Find out what they need, observe their interactions, and find ways to give them honest input. Look for trusted sources who will tell you what is being said about you when you're not in the room so you can make course corrections.

SUMMARY:
What We Want You to Know

- Once you've established where you want to go, guidance and course corrections will help you arrive more quickly.

- Remember that people's perceptions of you are their reality. Take them seriously.

- Feedback and action can help influence and change others' perceptions.

- Proactively seek advice and feedback, then decide on a course of action. Thank those who offer you the gift of feedback, and if appropriate, report back to them on the actions you've taken.

- Alter others' perceptions by taking strong action and using self-promotion. Talk about what you're learning and the changes you've made.

- Learn to make feedback your friend. Spend time thinking about it and allow it to help you grow.

CHAPTER FIVE

Missing the Point of Preparation

Be Strategic about the Outcome You Want

The amateur works until they can get it right. The professional works until they can't get it wrong.

— UNKNOWN

Maya, a senior vice president for an asset management firm, was in charge of a major presentation to the executive committee. The company was planning a significant business expansion that would involve a hefty financial investment and consequential changes. For months, Maya and her team had been working almost nonstop on planning the execution. The team had dissected how the change would affect budgets, operations, staffing, and training and had outlined the transitions that would be required.

On the day of the presentation to the committee, Maya had perfected the data, charts, and slides that would explain the expansion plan. No detail had been overlooked. She was satisfied and proud that she and her team had produced a beautiful, informative report. She was confident that the hard work would pay off in a flawless presentation.

The day after her meeting, Maya had a coaching session with Kathryn. When Kathryn asked her how the presentation had gone, Maya ducked her head and slumped her shoulders, looking frustrated. The presentation hadn't had the impact she'd been hoping for and the project was stalled again.

As they deconstructed the meeting, Maya said that her time on the agenda had been cut in half. Although she knew the information inside and out, she hadn't been able to land strategic, focused points. Because board members had so many questions, time had run out and she didn't get a motion to support the plan and move the work forward. The delay in decision-making would cost the organization months. Maya told Kathryn she felt discouraged.

Kathryn asked about the ways she had prepared. Maya detailed the hard work she and her team had done: gathering data, producing documents, creating informative, professional slides. "Yes, but how did you prepare for the delivery of that information?" Kathryn asked. "Did you rehearse to account for timing and pace? Did you talk to board members or influencers before the meeting to see if they had questions or concerns? Were you prepared for possible resistance?"

Maya hadn't really practiced. She said that because of the depth of her expertise, she had felt prepared to make her presentation. The expansion had been on the agenda of several meetings, so she figured people were familiar with the issues. She was pretty good on her feet, she added, and didn't see the need to invest time in rehearsing formally or lining up support for a motion to move forward before the presentation.

Maya's story is just one strong example of women we often see who are "overworked and under-practiced." Preparation and practice, in our view, have a much broader scope than most women realize.

Women tell us far too often that their primary objective is "to get the work done." We're not here to tell you that's not important, but "doing the work" is only a part of getting the job done. The secret to preparation and practice is to first establish a strong vision for a desired outcome.

This can allow you to think more expansively about everything that needs to be done to achieve your goal. By becoming more strategic in this area, you optimize the chances of getting the successful outcomes you're looking for.

In our research and work with thousands of women, we have observed that the tendency to neglect this dimension of preparation is widespread. It's so common yet so subtle that we've dubbed it "the silent killer." When women spend disproportionate time "doing the work" and neglect adequate preparation and practice on the important surrounding issues, they suboptimize their leadership, influence, and relationships.

Preparation for a presentation, for example, entails far more than knowing the topic and who will be in the room. Laying the groundwork for true influence means carefully rehearsing, making phone calls, and scheduling conversations to find out in advance where others stand on key issues that influence decision-making. One woman we coached ultimately considered "counting the votes" a key preparation activity. She had learned that most important decisions get made before the meeting. "If you haven't done the work ahead of time, it is more likely to go the wrong way," she told us.

Ask people who perform for a living—athletes, actors, musicians—about practice and you're likely to get a detailed report on their routines. You'll hear about long hours in the gym doing specific drills or many hours practicing a complicated section of music. Athletes can tell you about their calorie intake and how it affects performance, actors can tell you how many weeks or months they need to absorb a character, and musicians can tell you details about rehearsals, practice, and lessons to master a particular technique. They are crystal clear about the outcome they seek, they visualize the results, and they know what specific tasks are required to achieve their goal. That discipline and ability to practice rituals make performances look natural and effortless. This can trick people into thinking that the task is easy. Performers know what we want you to know, that practice and preparation are key to maximizing impact, instilling confidence, and being successful.

A CEO we worked with shared a story about a leader she had observed and admired. She said he could "ignite the room" when he took the stage at large employee meetings. "He was so smooth and inspiring in front of hundreds of people," she told us. "It looked and felt so natural." She wanted to know how he did it. How was he able to come out of a day filled with meetings and stress and then jump up in front of his organization and be so electric? Eventually, she had the opportunity to ask him, "How do you do that so easily?" He looked at her intently and replied, "It is *not* easy. It doesn't come naturally. I work really hard at it. It comes from creating the stories and rehearsing them over and over. I continually work to make improvements." His secret wasn't an inherited talent, it was his relentless practice that kept an outcome at the forefront of his work.

As a professional on a different type of stage or playing field, your craft should include clarifying your intention, visualizing your outcome, digesting relevant information, creating a compelling message, and knowing your audience. But even that is not enough.

The hard work of rehearsing and fine tuning is the key to a brilliant performance that feels natural, authentic, and powerful.

THE BLIND SPOT: NOT UNDERSTANDING THE BROAD SCOPE OF PREPARATION AND PRACTICE

When women we coach are upset or distressed about something that did not go well in their work, we usually discover that they've invested too little time in preparation or practice. Their tendency is to focus on getting the numbers right, gathering the information, and nailing down the processes. They leap from planning to execution instead of making several small, essential jumps along the way. This is another blind spot.

You can offset this blind spot by setting an intention and establishing a high-intensity clarity about the outcomes you seek. Questions such as, "How do I want to show up?" "What do I want from others?" "What impact do I need to deliver?" "If everything went well, what would happen?" can be game changers. The ability to clearly visualize and talk about a preferred outcome is a hallmark of highly effective leaders (and ideally you). Visualize. Plan. Practice.

Clarity, planning, and practice foster confidence. As we say often to the women we coach: "Confidence is a set of behaviors, it's not a feeling." Preparation and practice lead to the ultimate state of confidence—that feeling that you cannot get it wrong. In that place, a lot of good can happen.

Sometimes women neglect this step because they're unaware of its importance or they feel too busy to focus on it, but we often find something else at play—avoidance. Telling yourself that you're "good on your feet" or that "doing the work" is preparation enough can be a way of deflecting the pressure and stress of performing. But devoting time to practicing, preparing, and rehearsing has incremental and often monumental impact. *Intense preparation is not to be underestimated.*

Hard work is essential, of course, because it's your ticket to a seat at the table. But mastering the storyline and clearly articulating your messages deserve as much time as you devote to your job's technical aspects. Women cannot afford to wing it, as Maya did, in their quest for impact. Precise, relentless practice for presentations in settings that range from routine meetings to major presentations can help you sell ideas, influence decision-making, and optimize successful outcomes. It will provide opportunities to shine and will help you thrive in your career. If you do not address this blind spot, the risk of diminished personal power is high.

THE PERILS OF THE BLIND SPOT

One woman we coached described how exhausted she was from running to back-to-back meetings almost every day. In a coaching session, Brenda asked: "What impact do you want or expect to have in these forums? How do you prepare for meetings? How many truly need your presence?" After analyzing the situation, eventually our client was able to reclaim several hours of her work week. Many meetings didn't require her presence, and she could still add value by sending a note or making a call to the leader to share her input or suggestions.

How often do you rush into a meeting without knowing the real agenda? How much do you know about the decision-makers and influencers and your role in the meeting? Is the meeting for exposure, for input, or for making decisions to proceed? Without preparation, you won't know what questions need to be asked or be ready with a point of view and insightful comments. If you don't prepare and practice, your overarching themes and key points are in danger of being obscured by interruptions or a lack of focus. Even without meaning to, it's easy to end up in the weeds.

While you might get away with faking it or flying by the seat of your pants for a while, failing to prepare and practice is bound to catch up with you. At the very least, it can delay or stall an upward career trajectory. There are at least four dangers that come from neglecting the two important "P" words of career building—preparation and practice.

Bombing

This not only will affect you personally, it also will take away from the impact of an idea or project. Bombing ranges from completely losing your footing during a performance (a meeting discussion, a presentation, or a crucial conversation with a colleague) to not achieving necessary or preferred work outcomes. It takes time and effort to regroup, recover, and get back on track after bombing. It's draining.

Losing Your Audience

In many respects, this is people's worst nightmare, and no one sets out to do it on purpose. Even if you don't lose people entirely, it is possible that your audience might take to your ideas but think you are not the best person to lead them to the next level.

Marginalizing Yourself

Suboptimizing your impact can have long-lasting negative effects on the goals you've established, the trajectory of your work, and on your reputation. Diminishing personal power can be a derailer. The feedback we hear about many women is that they need a strong point of view and a clear voice in discussions, whether in specific meetings or throughout the process of work in one-on-one conversations or in smaller group discussions.

Never Getting Better

Women who practice and prepare on purpose become better. They appear more confident and exude presence. Lack of focus and poor preparation inevitably lead to missed opportunities: a promotion denied, not being named to an important project, or getting a performance review that identifies you as someone who is not developing. Practice will build your skills and muscle memory and you will get better with every iteration.

Preparation and practice can infuse your work with energy and create confidence that boosts your impact. Choreographer Martha Graham was emphatic about the significance of practice. She wrote:

> *I believe that we learn by practice. Whether it means to learn to dance by practicing dancing or to learn to live by practicing living, the principles are the same. In each, it is the performance of a dedicated, precise set of acts, physical or intellectual, from which comes the shape of achievement, a sense of one's being, a satisfaction of spirit. Practice means to perform, over and over again, in the face of all obstacles, some act of vision, of faith, of desire. Practice is a means of inviting the perfection desired.[1]*

COACH ON YOUR SHOULDER
Questions to Help You Reflect on Where You Are Now

- What missed opportunities in your career have come from lack of preparation and practice? How will you do things differently?
- What do-over would you like to practice so that you could achieve a different outcome?
- How can you get clear about a desired outcome, whether it is for a meeting or a presentation or a career?
- Get curious about how the best in your field or in other industries prepare and practice. What are their routines, rituals, and areas of focus?
- How will you find ways to get feedback on your practice and rehearsals so you can fine-tune?
- What small thing can you do to better prepare for meetings and get your voice into the room?

STRATEGIES

Preparation and practice can be built into a daily work routine (figure 8). Get it on your calendar!

Build in rehearsal time when you have a big presentation coming up. Make time to review a meeting agenda and jot down your perspective, comments, and questions. Be ready to contribute in any forum, whether you are presenting or not and even when the agenda isn't specifically related to your expertise or accountability.

This is about your goals, your commitment, and the end result. If you cannot see it and practice and prepare for it, then no one else will see it for you. Opportunities abound for honing your preparation and practice skills.

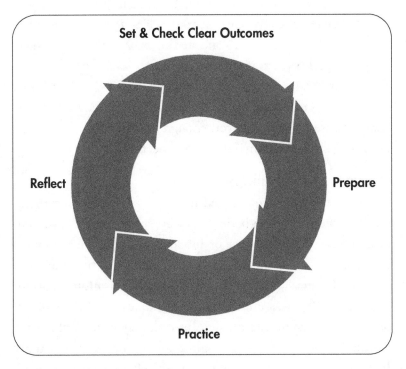

Figure 8. Preparation and practice cycle

Meetings

Get the agenda in advance and think about why you're attending. If you cannot imagine why you need to be there, can you decline the meeting, delegate, or follow up in some other way? If you are going to attend, go with intention and show up prepared. Have a list of concise points you want to make. Jot down questions you have.

Speak Up

Years of feedback on women leaders shows they are less likely to actively get their voices into the room when decisions are being made. There are many reasons you will need to work to make your voice heard, including being interrupted and talked over or having your idea reiterated by someone else as something new. An article Kathryn co-wrote titled "Women, Find Your Voice" highlights the challenges and gives women strategies for being heard in meetings.[2] Asking questions and sharing experience and perspectives are good ways to get heard. Introverts who are uncomfortable about speaking up need to think ahead. Decide in advance how you want to use your voice. Speaking early in the meeting can take pressure off and give you enough confidence to bring your perspective into the room later in the meeting.

Informal Conversations

Many women we have coached tell stories about finding themselves in the coffee line beside a key executive or randomly running into a decision-maker or influencer in the hallway or the elevator. One client was riding in an elevator with her company's chief legal counsel, someone who had important information she needed. But she was unprepared and couldn't think of a way to broach the topic in that setting. Instead, they chatted about the weather and sports for thirty-eight floors—a missed opportunity. In contrast, another client used a two-block walk for coffee with the CFO to get her topic on the next leadership agenda, eliminating weeks of back-and-forth protocol with his staff.

Dinners

Whether meals are for business purposes or personal, they can be a great way to connect with people on a different level. Think in advance about topics that might be of interest to everyone, such as a book, a movie, or travel recommendations. Think about work topics such as a new report or article you've read or a client you met with and learned something interesting from. How might you get people to engage more deeply? A little preparation makes it easier to leave a big impression.

Networking Events

We don't know many people who eagerly look forward to these. But with a little deliberate focus, creating or deepening relationships at such events can be rewarding. Show up with a purpose. One woman made it a goal to have conversations with two people she knew and two she didn't know before making her exit. Enlist a colleague or friend and make a pact to introduce each other to people. Prepare a few conversation starters. One of our favorites: "Tell me your story."

Board Meetings and Board Members

Research can help you know a little about who they are and what they care about. What is their background and experience? Start with a clear intention of what you'd like to see happen. Your intention drives everything. Do you want to get support for a key project? Make a case for a new initiative? Clarify how upcoming changes will affect your division? What data and information will help you make your case and enlist others to your cause? Prepare questions or a key message you'd like to share.

Interviews

Many women find themselves deep into their careers before they need to interview formally again. Over time, you've likely advanced into new roles or your current role has evolved. Organizational shifts can mean new leadership and support systems, and you might find you need to defend your position—or opt for a new one. Consider how your accomplishments, perspectives, and stories have changed, then practice by injecting them into conversations with key leaders or prospective employers. Create opportunities to tout yourself as a valuable employee or new hire. Create an intentional, masterful way of telling your story and rehearse until confident behaviors prevail. Talk about the *results* you have achieved—revenue goals, new customer acquisition, cycle time reduction, or other results related to your role.

Coaching an Employee

Get clear about the intention of your conversation, specific points that need to be made, and the best way to make them. What is the business case for asking people to change their behavior or do things differently? Ask yourself, "What do I need to accomplish and how do I want this person to feel at the end of our conversation?"

Making a Big Ask

Women are great about asking for things for others in order to take care of their teams or colleagues. It can be nerve-wracking to ask for yourself. Construct a business case and be direct, concise, and impactful by honing and practicing your request. Think through the solutions you want to see, consider how you'll respond to resistance, and always end with agreement about next steps.

Hone Your Point of View

Ground your perspectives about business needs with homework. What is the cost-benefit analysis of developing in-house expertise versus outsourcing? Should the group fund or defund a project?

Expand or exit a market? If your message gets lost in the chatter, look for a way to repeat it or underscore it in different ways. Sharpening your perspective, communicating it, and debating it are marks of a prepared, confident leader.

Review Successes

One of the hallmarks of highly impactful leaders is setting aside consistent time to think about accomplishments and what happened that created success. Consider your biggest challenges and how you navigated them. Create stories about your achievements and make yourself the hero. This is why athletes watch game tapes the day after and why actors review their performances. They are looking for what worked and how to replicate it.

STORIES THAT HOLD US BACK

When we coach women about the importance of preparation and practice, we notice two main responses—no time to do it and/or anxiety. Women say things such as:

> "I'm better off if I don't have too much time to think about it. Otherwise, I get stage fright."

> "Doing my work doesn't leave time for practice or rehearsing."

> "I don't really know how to rehearse."

> "Some people are naturally good at presenting or talking to groups. That's just not me."

> "I don't have the time."

> "At my level, I feel like I'm already supposed to know what I'm doing."

> "I can't get my energy if I'm too scripted."

> "I do better when I improvise. I'm good on my feet."

The last couple of points were arguments made by one client, Sonia. Her belief was that too much practice and preparation would diminish spontaneity and make her feel forced, too formal, and less authentic. She emphatically explained that she was best "on her feet" and intentionally chose not to invest time, effort, or energy in fine-tuning.

However, she had an "Aha!" moment during a talk she gave to the division she had recently been assigned to lead that consisted of several thousand employees across the globe. Many were in the audience and others joined the meeting virtually from their home bases.

Sonia was no stranger to the stage, and she enjoyed the spotlight. She typically found ways to communicate her vision and used humor and stories to connect with the audience and convey her messages. On the day of the speech, she began with her usual energy. But something strange happened during her opening remarks. Sonia felt as if she were going to collapse. Her mouth became dry and her breathing erratic. She reached for water again and again. She powered through and retreated to her office to collapse and recover.

When she later talked with her coach, she said this feeling of collapse had happened in her last few public talks. Because she had completed her speech, she didn't think anyone noticed what was happening with her. But something was wrong, and she was worried about herself.

Her coach watched the video of the meeting, and in the first two minutes, it was clear what was happening. Sonia wasn't breathing. She started out in her fast-talking, energetic style, trying to exude enthusiasm to the new people in her division. But Sonia's previous public speeches had been for audiences of 50 to 100 people, and her typical techniques weren't really scalable for the thousands of people who were listening in person and online. She needed to prepare differently—and intentionally practice—a refined message and delivery.

Sonia was relieved to learn that she was underpracticed rather than ill, and she went to work. She began a disciplined rehearsal routine that helped her find a better rhythm for the large audiences she was addressing. She learned a better balance of breathing and pausing for emphasis while maintaining her humor and sincere style.

People who work for companies often don't consider practice to be something they need to do at work. Practice seems like something for people who perform for a living. As Martha Graham's quote aptly points out, though, all aspects of life benefit from practice. You practice with focus on the desired outcome, establishing a cadence and special rituals and habits that help you get it right while feeling confident and comfortable.

THE POWER OF REFRAMING: NEW STORY

A new CEO, Frances, was about to have her first meeting with the company's board of directors. She had constructed a solid agenda and lined up the necessary documents and subject-matter experts for presentations. During a coaching session, Kathryn asked: "How are you planning to kick off this meeting? How do you want to land with this new audience?" Silence.

Finally, Frances opened up. She was feeling anxious about the meeting. She had not given much thought about her approach or how she could facilitate the meeting in a purposeful way. She wasn't clear about her perspectives. Kathryn suggested that they rehearse. Together, they talked through her vision for the outcome and practiced the meeting transitions. Francis formulated a plan for moving from one topic to the next, what she wanted to get out of each discussion, and how she would close the meeting.

After the meeting, Frances reported she'd felt in control through-out the four-hour session and was extremely pleased with the outcome. The preparation and practice had paid off, as had her reflection about Kathryn's final questions during their coach-ing sessions: "If the meeting were to go really well, what would that look like? What would happen, what would you be doing?" Preparing for her vision of an end result made all the difference. Being intentional and taking the time to prepare and practice for a great performance gave her a solid landing and contrib-uted to successfully accomplishing the goals of the meeting.

Kathryn knew about the power of intention from first-hand experience. As the leader of a large training and development division, she was on tap to give a high-stakes presentation to sev-eral hundred new employees who had come into the organization after an acquisition. She knew the audience might not be friendly to her message, so she visualized the goal of her presentation. "As I sorted through it, I got clear that I wanted to get people fired up," Kathryn said. "I wanted them to be engaged and to focus on the end game." She decided she wanted to get applause at two specific points in her presentation to signify approval, so she designed her talk around messages that would achieve this. Clear about her intention, Kathryn prepared and rehearsed with her outcome in mind. It worked. They applauded in the right places. They left the meeting energized. "Had I not spent the time on exactly what I wanted to happen and worked hard to achieve it," she said, "the meeting easily could have derailed or just been OK."

You are a performer like actors and athletes and musicians; you just have a different discipline, venue, and stage. By crafting an authentic message, you can become an effective storyteller. What might change if you viewed preparation for your work forums as a kind of performance that was essential to practice?

Tim Grover, a trainer for athletic greats like Michael Jordan and the late Kobe Bryant, hammers hard the importance of persistence in his book *Relentless*. Grover recounts how Bryant worked on even the smallest details of his craft so he could look effortless on the court when it counted. He repeated basic drills over and over every day, improving his strength and agility through repetition. Grover says "relentless" describes the most intense competitors and achievers, those who are exceedingly clear about what the end result looks like and feels like. They put in the necessary, consistent, repetitious work to achieve it.[3]

In the business world, practice is more than just standing up in front of a mirror and talking or quickly reading through a talk or presentation right before you deliver it. Focused practice, maybe with a colleague or trusted friend to give you feedback, is a way to make sure you will articulate your messages clearly and confidently and anticipate snags or questions.

Consider replacing the old stories and beliefs with new self-talk:

"I can get clear on my outcomes."

"I can know what to prepare and practice for specific events at work."

"I don't have to practice everything all at once."

"When I'm prepared, I am clear, confident, and present."

Ruth came to a coaching session with Brenda one day feeling stressed about a divisionwide, all-hands meeting she was to host in the week ahead. She felt so overwhelmed that she had almost canceled her coaching session. As the new leader of the division, she was not looking forward to the meeting. She told

Brenda it was too early to share specific plans or organizational changes. She had decided she would just introduce herself and then take questions.

Brenda asked about her vision for her new role and the scheduled meeting. How well did she know the individuals on the team? Did she know if they shared her dreams? Were they happy to have a leader who could advance work that had already begun? What might happen if she used the meeting to engage people in ideas and enroll them in the start of a new leadership epoch?

After the discussion, Ruth sounded more energized and her attitude about the meeting had shifted. She was committed to an outcome of exciting and engaging her new division and began to prepare with that vision in mind. She called her direct reports ahead of time and asked them about their challenges and ideas. Instead of winging it, Ruth crafted a focused, more interesting introduction of herself. She prepared her comments and, enlisting her coach, rehearsed key messages.

A few weeks later, Ruth reported back. The meeting had been an invigorating, engaging session where ideas and experiences were exchanged. She felt confident, energized, and open after hearing buzz that her team was talking about their refreshing new leader. People saw her as present, clear, and creative. The group even started using a mantra that captured the team's purpose. They were off to a great start.

Instead of wasting time worrying about the meeting and imagining disaster, Ruth visualized a better outcome and spent time deliberately thinking about the impact she wanted to make, then taking aim at her target. The preparation and practice gave her a confidence boost and the meeting affirmed her leadership abilities.

COACH ON YOUR SHOULDER
Tips for Steering Clear of the Blind Spot

VISUALIZE THE OUTCOME Every highly effective person we have coached focuses on, defines, and conveys the outcome they want. They can see it and describe it in vivid detail. They prepare and rehearse with that clear picture in mind.

MAKE A LIST Elaborate on the ways you can practice for meetings, phone calls, and informal conversations. Study meeting topics and the attendee list ahead of time. If there is no agenda, ask the leader about its purpose and key topics. Getting ruthless with your schedule is crucial. As we say to the women we coach, saying no to certain things enables you to say yes to something more important.

PRACTICE YOUR POINT OF VIEW Be ready with observations, comments, and questions so you're always ready to contribute. Decide in advance what you believe, where you might compromise, and where you will not budge. Determine up front how to respond to negative or challenging points of view and where you need more information.

LINE UP VOTES As best you can, know the outcome going in to a big meeting or discussion. A book Kathryn co-wrote, *The Influence Effect*, outlines a full strategy for lining up votes and influencing others.[4] One woman we coach said this habit made her more aware of the views of others and how things might work better if she incorporated them. Investing time in these conversations helped her understand business challenges and establish deeper, trusting relationships with people she might otherwise view as adversaries.

REHEARSE IN CHUNKS Stage and film actors rehearse in blocks, focusing deeply on a specific area of the performance. A violinist will work on a particularly difficult passage for hours. This works for business professionals, too. In her book *Before You Say Anything*, Angie Flynn-McIver recommends this approach. She emphasizes working on your introduction in one setting.[5] In another session, practice transitions from one topic to another. Rehearse the closing separately. Put it all together in several final practices before "show time." Make it work for your style and schedule. For example, some like to practice segments while drying their hair or driving or working out. This works particularly well for practicing stories and examples or transitions in a speech.

PHONE A FRIEND Look for a mentor or knowledgeable colleagues who will give you targeted feedback. Tell them specifically what you want: "I'm working on an impactful opening. I want you to tell me how it lands or give me pointers on how to improve." When others know what to look for and what you're after, they are in a better position to help. We coach women to prop up their phone on the desk and record themselves delivering parts of their presentation or an update they'll be delivering in a virtual meeting. Video or voice recordings give you real-time feedback on pace, emphasis of points, posture, gestures, and the built-in pause. Recording even routine updates can help you fine-tune word choices or pace.

These are skills you can build. Clarity about intentions and outcomes and working on delivery with focused repetition will get you from the place beyond just getting it right to that ultimate state of "can't get it wrong."

SUMMARY:
What We Want You to Know

- Doing your job is essential and you need to match that with preparation and practice.

- Professionals, whether they are athletes, actors, musicians, or corporate leaders, are always working to get better at their craft. Be that professional.

- Before you begin practicing, get clear about your intentions and the outcome you want.

- Preparation includes developing a perspective and being ready to contribute comments and questions in meaningful, positive ways.

- Practicing so that you cannot get it wrong leads to confidence, influence, and personal power.

CHAPTER SIX

Trying to Go It Alone

Assemble a Posse

If you want to go quickly, go alone. If you want to go far, go together.

— UNKNOWN

Natalie was silent. Kathryn could almost hear her scouring her brain, searching for an answer to the simple question: "Who might you talk to?" Natalie kept coming up blank.

Although she reported to the C-suite at a large financial services company, Natalie, who was in her early 40s, was aiming higher. She aspired to land in the C-suite. She had been offered a promotion that might move her closer to that objective, but it was in a different department than the one she currently worked for. It would mean operating outside her area of expertise, not to mention outside her comfort zone. Natalie also worried that the steep learning curve and extra workload might affect how she managed her life outside work. Given those factors, she was struggling to decide whether it was the right move.

"I don't know what to do," Natalie told Kathryn. "I'm unclear about what the risks and the rewards are." Kathryn asked Natalie who she might turn to for advice in making this pivotal decision. "Well, I can talk to you," Natalie said. "I guess I could talk to my boss. Or maybe a girlfriend—but she doesn't know my skills or experience at work."

Kathryn kept pressing. Who else? Might there be a helpful colleague whom she could trust? A former college professor or mentor who could advise her? A family member? A peer in a similar or different industry? Anyone she had met at professional conferences? A former colleague who had helped her in a previous job or role?

Natalie could only think of one or two people—and that was a problem.

BLIND SPOT: NO WOMAN IS AN ISLAND

Many women are so focused on their daily responsibilities and "getting the job done" that they haven't developed and fostered what we affectionately call "a posse." This is a serious blind spot, because such a group gives women vast, valuable resources for being more effective at work and help in steering their careers.

We use the term posse to describe a helpful web of work connections and other relationships with people who can provide reliable information, support, and advice. Your posse can be enormously helpful to your ability to "get the job done." This means finding people you can turn to for help about deciding whether to take on a project at work, for advice about how to get your voice heard in meetings, for suggestions on better ways to juggle career and home. Members of your posse are the thought partners who can weigh in when you're trying to figure out whether to join a task force or create a committee, how to sell an idea, or decide whether the promotion would be a good career move. When you're struggling and feeling like you might sink, your posse is there to throw you a lifeline. When life feels overwhelming, your posse stands ready to lend a helping hand. Having that kind of support can save your sanity.

The women we have coached have called having a posse a game changer because the members of their group provide a supportive foundation that allows them to thrive—and equally important, sustain—long careers. A healthy roster of sponsors, mentors, colleagues, friends, and family members who can expand your thinking, offer assistance, and cheer you on will enable you to achieve your career goals more easily and efficiently.

PERILS OF THE BLIND SPOT

In our coaching practice, we often see women struggling to cultivate a career without enough help and support. You cannot go it alone and have a highly impactful career. If you want to maximize your potential, it's important to recognize this and develop the ability to ask for what you need. You can have a career without a posse, but you are likely to get farther, be more successful, and feel less stressed with a team on your side.

Not having a posse puts you in a less advantageous position at work. Here are some of the dangers of going it alone that we've identified:

Missed Opportunities

Systems analysts Yang Yang, Nitesh V. Chawla, and Brian Uzzi have found that a key indicator of success in women's career trajectory is a close inner circle of women. While networking is important to both genders, women and men typically use their networks in different ways. When discussing job interviews and workplace concerns, women often want to know how an organization's culture affects women, and "that type of information is most helpful if it comes from other women," says Brian Uzzi. Yang, Chawla, and Uzzi surmise that these small "inner networks" open up opportunities and allow for the exchange of advice focused on the specific challenges women face.[1] Although all genders benefit from broad networks, the most successful women have also cultivated a separate, smaller inner circle of trusted women they are close to.[2]

Not Having a Broad Base of Supporters

In *The Career Architect Development Planner*, Robert Eichinger and Michael Lombardo point out that overdependence on a single advocate can be a career derailer.[3] If you're too closely aligned with one sponsor or advocate, you might be seen as lacking independence, self-reliance, or power. And if something should happen to your sponsor, no one else might be aware of your capabilities and value, know your skills and potential, or be available to speak up on your behalf. Maria, one of our clients, found herself in that situation. She had moved up through the ranks at a large national manufacturing company, eventually landing a high-profile executive job as treasurer and head of investments. The CEO had been Maria's longtime sponsor and had complete faith in her. But after he was diagnosed with cancer and had to suddenly leave his job, the company's leadership regime changed. Maria found herself with no posse, no colleagues, and no leaders who could step up to attest to the value she added and offer reasons why it was important that she retain her role. When the new leadership team took over, Maria was swept out. If you have only one sponsor, your fortunes can quickly spiral downward if something happens to him or her.

Lack of Information

While working in the banking industry, Brenda relied on someone who was one of "the most connected people I ever knew" as she navigated her career. This woman made it her business to know what was going on—who was getting promoted, which new products were being vetted, and what new client relationships were emerging. She was a connector who listened closely to what other people knew and, more important, shared knowledge with others. Being in a meeting with her was like reading a newsletter. Even though Brenda knew she was never going to be exactly like this well-connected woman, she recruited her as a key member of her posse. The relationship continues today. "She's given me great advice over the years and she's still super good to talk to," Brenda says. Look to recruit people to your posse who are sailing on the flow of information and idea generation. They are invaluable. Your posse should include people who look out for you and who scan the horizon for potential projects, promotions, and possibilities. Once they know what you want and need, they can spot and alert you to opportunities that might fit and/or advocate for you.

Lack of Career Navigation

Most of the women we work with are knowledge workers who are employed in organizations where the career ladder isn't a straight line. A lot of white space exists in today's complex, matrixed, leveraged organizations, and you need more brains than the one in your cranium to root out the best ways to move upward and achieve career goals. Today's career path is unlikely to be linear or logical. If you have strong relationships, you're more likely to hear about the deals that are being made, business trends, mergers, reorganizations, job openings, and disruptive technologies. This information can help you figure out how and where to steer your career.

Running Out of Gas

We've coached many women who are burned out. For too long, they've been fighting career headwinds as solo sailors, trying to get where they want to go without a knowledgeable crew. A supportive circle of people can prop you up when frustration and fatigue begin to boil over, when challenges pile up in a way that feels insurmountable. In one memorable coaching call, our exhausted, demoralized client talked about losing sleep over a tough job situation in which she was trying her utmost to protect the team she managed. She did not feel supported and felt very much alone. The resources she needed to take care of herself seemed absent. Her life was consumed by the job, and she became so overwhelmed in the coaching conversation that she cried. Her tank was empty—she'd run out of gas.

Burnout can make you feel like there is nowhere to turn. Research bolsters this assertion.[4] This became even more clear during the COVID-19 pandemic, when we all learned that consistent self-care and support from other people can make the difference between doing well, hanging in, or spiraling down. Studies show that one way to foster resilience and avoid burnout is to develop strong social support systems.[5]

Interacting Only with People Who Are Like You

It's natural to drift toward people you have a lot in common with, but that can present an obstacle to learning and new experiences. It's important that you don't surround yourself with people who look at the world exactly the way you do or share your personality traits. Members of your posse should have different styles, backgrounds, points of view, and knowledge and should have other traits than you do. Fresh outlooks from people who can expand your thinking are very important. One woman we worked with allied herself with a colleague who had the ability to stay calm and methodical under pressure. She wasn't easily rattled, and our client recruited her to her posse because she was eager to develop that capacity. Many of us grew up with people who are a lot like we are. If you develop relationships with people who have different knowledge, skills, competencies, cultural backgrounds, perspectives, and personalities and learn about the ways they approach things, you can augment your learning opportunities. In addition, scholarly research supports the idea that diverse groups make better decisions.[6]

Remembering Who You Are

The rewards of a posse can go far beyond career development. You need people who can help you remember who you are when things get rough, who can re-center you when you start wondering why you made the choices you did. For example, after a long, successful career in banking during which Brenda helped financial organizations improve their customers' experiences, she got a call from a former colleague who had joined the U.S. Department of Education under Arne Duncan, secretary of education during the Obama administration. They wanted her to become the first chief customer experience officer and asked her to change the culture of student lending. While the invitation was flattering and customer service was her sweet spot, Brenda had never considered a job in the public sector. But in further conversations, she connected with the vision. She wanted to make a difference in the lives of younger people and this position provided a platform to do that. Although Brenda took the job, she worried about losing sight of why she was going to Washington D.C. She turned to her posse to prop her up when she felt discouraged and questioned what she was doing and why she had taken the job. They stepped up on many occasions to help her reconnect with her purpose. Without them, Brenda says, she couldn't have been as productive and as satisfied in her new role. And although she eventually left that post, she continues to tap into the wisdom and support of her posse today.

Remembering who you are is also necessary when you need to let go and reinvent yourself. During reinvention, the doubting days when you wonder whether you're doing the right thing are bound to come along. Your courage to do something different will get tested. In the midst of making a wanted or needed shift, your posse can give you the affirmation you need to stay grounded and on course.

COACH ON YOUR SHOULDER
Questions to Help You Reflect on Where You Are Now

- Who do you trust to help you navigate your career and how can you enroll them in your posse?
- What is holding you back from getting people to help you?
- What new step will you take to focus on creating your support network?
- How can you demonstrate reciprocity with the people in your posse?
- What will you do to create time and space to develop and maintain relationships?

STRATEGIES

Building relationships with purpose and focus is a great career advantage. Start with a list. Write down anyone you can think of who has the potential to be a contributing member of your team. Think about the people you trust, people who are in the know, people who have helped you get things done, or people who have influenced your thinking or behavior. Peruse your social media accounts for people you've connected with who are potential members of the posse you need.

Based on your list, start populating categories with the people you have identified (see figure 9). Remember, posse relationships can overlap—it's not only fine to have people who occupy more than one category on your list, it can be an advantage. What's most essential is finding and cultivating people who are in a position to help, advise, and support you and who you can give to reciprocally. Look for people who can fill a variety of roles as you navigate your career. In this section, we discuss each of the categories that you see in figure 9.

A "Board of Directors"

Don't worry. We're not talking about the highly paid people who run companies, worry about shareholders, and hire and fire CEOs. This is a metaphor, not a formal group that meets to make decisions. However, it can be invaluable to assemble a group of diverse people with varying expertise that you can turn to when you need guidance or direction. These should be people who know you well, who understand your challenges, and who maybe even feel like stakeholders in your success. They don't even necessarily have to know each other. They are only like a corporate board in the sense that you can ask them hard questions and they can help you with strategy because they know you, they know your situation, and they know the organization.

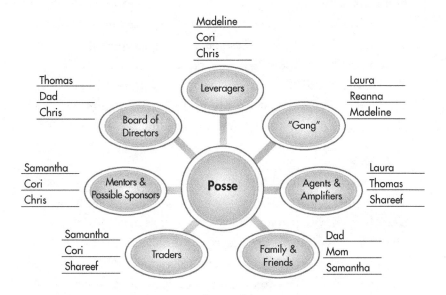

Figure 9. Find your people

Sponsors

Sponsors are people who will go to bat for you. They are willing to expend political capital to put you on a critical project team, identify leadership opportunities, or insist that you get that promotion. Organizational behaviorist Herminia Ibarra points to research showing that men have sponsors in much higher numbers than women.[7] If the notion of a sponsor makes you feel like you're powerless or overly dependent, think of them as connectors and advocates. They want to help because they know the value you bring. We worked with one woman who had a strong sponsor high up in her organization. When he was asked for names to consider for a senior leadership promotion, he immediately identified this woman. "Can you give me other names?" he was asked. "No," he replied firmly. "Trust me. She is the only name you need."

Agents or Promoters

These are people who can actively market you. They will mention your name and talk you up to appropriate people. They'll be ready with solid reasons why you should be given projects and be considered for new roles. These people play a different role from a sponsor. They're more like your personal advertising agency, a cheerleader squad for your qualities and accomplishments. This also works in reverse: look for opportunities to promote the capable women you know. Create a virtuous cycle.

Mentors

These people are valued thought partners who are politically savvy and can give you solid advice. They're ready and willing to talk an issue through with you to help you consider as many angles as possible. Mentors can help you understand an organization's culture in a way that helps you avoid making unintentional gaffes or mistakes. Kathryn coached one woman, for example, who was seen by her peers as a hard driver. Many would see that as a good trait, but her style was out of sync with the organization's more collaborative culture. Once she got feedback from a mentor, the woman adjusted her work style to be more open and inclusive and she became more effective as a team player. An important point to keep in mind, though, is that women tend to be overmentored and underspon-sored.[8] As you build trust with your mentors, keep in mind that it might be possible to turn them into sponsors.

Amplifiers

Find mutually supportive women and talk about the ways you can work together to amplify your voices in meetings and other organizational arenas. When a trial balloon goes up during a meeting, help keep it up in the air by reiterating the idea, talking about its merits, and giving credit to the person who said it first. Find others who will do the same for you. This worked well for a group of women who had high-profile jobs at the White House during Obama's presidency. Their presence in the administration's inner circle was groundbreaking and important. Even so, they had to fight the unconscious gender bias that happens when many of the people in the room are men. The women allied with each other and adopted a strategy of repeating each other's ideas and comments, underscoring the name of the woman who made the original contribution. This not only helped the men recognize the women's contributions, it also prevented men from claiming the ideas as their own.[9] If you're the only woman at the table, see if you can enlist a male colleague in your effort.

People with Business Intelligence

People who have good business intelligence are valuable for help-ing you understand trends, navigate business currents, and make better decisions. We have one colleague who developed sources throughout her company and her industry. This breadth helped her gather a holistic picture of the business she worked in.

Traders

When Kathryn got a big promotion, she suddenly went from being a leadership development expert to overseeing training and development for the entire organization. This included divisions like operations, technology, and finance that she knew very little about. Knowing she needed to get knowledgeable fast, she called Janet, a woman she knew in operations. When Kathryn asked for help, Janet replied, "You know, I've been trying to get you to do some team development in the department for a long time." Kathryn agreed to make that a priority, and in exchange, Janet agreed to be her go-to person when Kathryn needed operations information or expertise. The exchange of service doesn't have to be exclusively with women. You're aiming for the ability to cultivate give-and-take that serves you and the other person and therefore the organization.

A "Gang"

Sometimes you just need a sympathetic ear and time to unload over a cup of coffee or a glass of wine. The members of your gang can be supportive women who are there for you when you need to let off a little steam, find fresh ideas, or create new coping strategies. They're the team that helps you deal with microaggressions at work, especially if you are one of only a few women in a senior leadership position. This network doesn't have to be strictly career-oriented, either. You're looking for friends who get it, who might jump in to help with childcare emergencies, insist you take a break when you're overwhelmed, and help you remember that you're not crazy. They'll take your "career 911" calls and then show up to help you sort it out.

Friends and Family

Don't forget about the people who love you and care about you, the ones you're closest with. Family and friends are already rooting for you, so why not tap into their love, support, and energy when yours is flagging? Sometimes the people who know you best can give you the most authentic feedback. When Kathryn was venting—again— about a difficult boss to her best friend one day, a simple question ("And were you *surprised* he acted that way?") provided an insight. The question helped Kathryn see that continually complaining about a boss who wasn't likely to change was not the best use of her time and energy. Enrolling your family and friends in your hopes and objectives helps them know how to support you. Share your successes and good days as well as your trials and frustrations.

Leveragers

Being overleveraged means you're taking on too much. That risks your ability to do great work and sustain it for the long haul. If you have the financial resources, don't let social expectations or guilt stop you from hiring the people who can make your life easier. Childcare providers, housekeepers, financial planners, tax preparers, restaurants with good takeout, and personal shoppers can help you leverage time and energy. Remember, your time is worth a lot. To whom can you delegate the things you don't have time for? It might make more financial sense to pay someone else if it helps free up time that allows you to focus on your career. We talk with too many women who are overworked, and not just because of their employment. Do what you do best and get others to help you with the rest.

STORIES THAT HOLD US BACK

In our coaching sessions, we hear the same statements over and over again:

> "I don't have time to build relationships, and even if I did, I don't have time to sustain them."

> "If I ask for help, I'm going to be seen as weak."

"The people who could really help me are too busy."

"I feel like it's contrived—like I'm just out for myself."

"Taking time to build a posse will distract me from the work I'm paid to do."

Fear can be a powerful obstacle when it comes to asking for help. Often women leaders tell us that they worry that asking for help will be seen as weakness or a sign that they're not confident about their decision-making skills. Many women we coach are what we call "onlys"; they are the only woman in a group of male colleagues. They want to fit in, and they use much of their energy trying to match the style of the dominant group and be accepted. They often don't realize the importance of tapping into the help of colleagues, allies, and other supporters.

Women are typically taught or have bought into a mythology that self-sufficiency is the ultimate virtue. They take to heart the saying "If you want something done right, do it yourself." They tend to ask for help or advice much less often than their male counterparts do. Such attitudes mean that women often don't view career building as the team sport that it is. Your career track will suffer if you're constantly swimming laps in the singles lane.

A lot of women in business back away from the word "network" because they hear a negative connotation. Many women we work with say that networking is "contrived" or "insincere" or "sounds too Machiavellian." Sometimes they'll just say, "I'm not good at networking." We find that reframing the term can be useful: networks are nothing more than a web of relationships. They range from casual to intimate and should be collegial, instructive, and mutually beneficial. We've discovered that when we talk to women about the importance of building relationships, they will say, "I'm good at that."

THE POWER OF REFRAMING: NEW STORY

In a professional assessment we did for Mary, a woman in her 30s who worked for a large insurance company, person after person talked about how well connected she was in the company and the industry. Colleagues said things like, "She doesn't stay in her own silo. She has lots of colleagues in the organization and lots of contacts outside the company. She has contacts throughout the industry. She knows how things get done and how to get things done." People saw her ability to develop and foster relationships and the way she leveraged them as a great strength.

When Brenda asked Mary how she had become so successful in this area, she said it started when she went to university. As a student on scholarship, Mary quickly realized that she needed to leverage every resource she could think of if she was going to be successful. She recognized early on she would need many diverse people on her team to help her achieve her academic goals. Mary carried that attitude over to her career. After graduation, the relationships she had developed in her academic life helped her land her first job and she continued to use her posse as her career advanced.

You can replace limiting beliefs by reframing your attitudes about asking for help. Recruiting people to your posse won't just help you, it can provide great benefits to others. Consider these points:

It Is Okay to Ask for Help

It can feel vulnerable to make a request, especially if you fear—consciously or unconsciously—that asking for help makes you appear weak. But doing so can also be a sign of strength and courage. You can ask for an introduction, for someone's point of view on a situation, for an assignment, or for help with getting your ideas out into the workplace. How will you know what help is available unless you ask? If someone says no, try not to take it personally and ask if he or she knows anyone else who might be in a position to help. Then try again—you might get a yes from someone else. Try more than once if it doesn't go well. We are big believers in trying more than once. Courage is a muscle that gets stronger the more you use it; the more you ask for help, the easier it gets.

Humility Is Overrated

Promoting yourself, talking about your goals and competencies, is a great way to help others know who you are and what you're reaching for. Talking with authenticity about what you're good at gives people information they could find useful. Point to some of your accomplishments and highlight your skills and competencies.

Get clear about your goals and look for opportunities to talk about them as a way of giving people the opportunity to advise and assist. People can't help if they don't know where you want to end up. Be clear about your requests. Clarity helps those who want to help you know exactly what kinds of information and opportunities you will find useful.

Asking Gives People an Opportunity to Be Generous

Turning to others for support and advice signals that you're human, open, and willing to grow. It also allows others to be generous. Asking for help and giving it shows that you know who you are and who you are not. And allowing other people to help you, inviting them to be a part of your inner circle, can prove to be a source of satisfaction for others. Think about it this way: why would you rob people of an opportunity to be of service?

If you haven't yet realized the power of the posse, take heart. It's never too late to start. Let's explore ways to find your people.

COACH ON YOUR SHOULDER
Advice for Steering Clear of the Blind Spot

STAY IN TOUCH Too many women we coach are embarrassed to realize that they haven't devoted time to keeping in touch with people in their web of relationships. This comes to light in a stark way when they need help to find another job or connect with a prospect or some other kind of help. Touch base occasionally to keep relationships alive with a note, an email, a text, a quick phone call, or a voicemail. Don't wait until you need something to reach out.

CONSTANTLY UPDATE YOUR LIST If you're just starting, a small, curated list is useful for building the posse. Make a phone call, suggest a meeting for coffee or lunch, send a friendly email. Make a point of having a focused conversation with a colleague. Let people know you're looking for help and assure them that you're eager to reciprocate. As your career develops, your list should expand. Constantly scan your environment to find people you can connect with in a beneficial, mutually supportive way. As you make or review your list, ask questions. Is there diversity among the members of your posse? Does it include younger and older people, people of different genders and ethnicities? Do they all know each other? (It's better if they don't.) Will members of your posse give you the information and support you need to be successful? Keep adding people—fresh faces mean fresh insights.

TRAVEL THE TWO-WAY STREET Relationships need attending to, just like houseplants or gardens. It's important to keep up with people. Check in regularly with your people to see what they're doing and how you can help. Women sometimes say, "I can't call someone out of the blue after so many years!" Why not? If it feels awkward, look for reasons to reach out. What is important to these people?

Have you seen an article that might be relevant to their work or life? Do you have a business referral for them? Have you seen (or can you find) news about them on social media or in an alumni newsletter? Do they have a blog or podcast you can comment on? Most people are happy to hear from people from their past, especially if the intention is to congratulate the person or to help them in some way.

ENROLL PEOPLE IN YOUR CAREER When you enrolled in school, you talked to your advisors, chose courses, checked out the professors, and asked for feedback on your assignments. Do this with your posse. Talk to people about your goals and challenges and ask for ideas and feedback. When you hit a milestone or make improvements based on the feedback you have received, circle back with an update to show that you value the help you received and that you're earnest about managing your career.

CREATE CALENDAR SPACE You'll greatly increase the chances of building and maintaining relationships if you set aside specific time on your calendar for making phone calls, writing a note, crafting an email, or sending texts. Keep "relationships" on your ongoing task list for those unexpected free times, such as when a meeting is canceled or an appointment is rescheduled. If your calendar or to-do list seems overcrowded, take a few minutes to jot down everything you think you need to do, whether it's work-related or buying new school supplies for the kids. Shed your Superwoman persona as you review the list. Ask, "What can I delegate? What can I delay? What can I delete?" This can help you free up time, replenish energy, and add perspective to your workload.

Again, a successful career is a team sport. Actively recruit your team, let them know what you want to do, and then let the team pitch in to help. Look for ways to help your team in return. Your career path will be smoother and your life will be full of an eclectic group of people who enrich your life.

SUMMARY:
What We Want You to Know

- Flying solo in your career is inefficient, exhausting, and unnecessary. You need more than a village if you want a thriving career that is sustainable. Find a "city" of people and build mutually beneficial relationships with them.

- Asking for help and giving it can be a great source of career power.

- Expand the way you think about building relationships. You want diversity among the people on your team of mentors, advisors, cheerleaders, and shoulders to lean on.

- Get clear about your capabilities and career goals and communicate them to people in your posse.

- Consciously cultivate your posse by scheduling time to stay in touch, help others, maintain long-term relationships, and build new ones.

CHAPTER SEVEN

Before We Go

The Deliberate Career

We could not close out this book without addressing the elephant in the room in every work environment, in every home. The elephant goes by many names these days—work-life balance or work-life synchronicity—but whatever you want to call it, it's something we all wrestle with. It's a recurring theme with most women we coach. Finding a way to integrate a career and your life outside work in a healthy way is the holy grail of our time. Volumes have been written about this issue, and in our rapidly changing world, this struggle will be ongoing.

If you're in the thick of it, remember that you are neither crazy nor alone. This book is about building capacity, creating confidence, and defining your direction, and we recognize that the opposing pulls from work and home colors all of that. It's an undercurrent that can push you off course or pull you under.

We have no easy solutions here—we wish we did. But this issue is too individualized to offer a broad panacea. We do believe this: in our experience and that of many others, a closer focus on the six blind spots and using the strategies for overcoming them is a way to give yourself some footing, grounding, capacity, and yes, even balance. *This is not about time management.* It is about commitments and boundaries and about being clear with yourself and others about both. It takes consistent, focused, committed practice.

Find the big and small strategies that work for you. Knowing what you want and where you're going is important—and equally important is knowing who you are and who you are not. Figure 10 includes our suggestions for practices and habits that can help you achieve more capacity and sanity.

CONCEPT	CONCRETE STEPS
Get clear about your values	Use a values assessment tool
Make commitments carefully	Audit your planner, schedule, or calendar
	Practice saying no
	Negotiate response time
Reframe your expectations	Look for new ways to get what you want in your home life
Create criteria for making decisions	Evaluate events and opportunities according to your values and priorities
Negotiate for flexibility	Ask for flexibility regarding work situations so you can have the quality of life you need
Ask for resources	Identify what you need to accomplish your goals and ask for those resources
Prioritize self-care	Make a list of what you need to be at your best and a list of things that drain you, then choose wisely
Gather your posse	Create a personal support network

Figure 10. Tools for a deliberate career

GET CLEAR ABOUT YOUR VALUES

Your values are the North Star in guiding your choices. If you're not sure how to define or articulate your values, many online assessments are available to help you examine and define what is most important to you. Search online using the term "values assessments" and find an assessment tool that resonates with you. Once you're clear about your core values, it's much easier to focus on what truly matters and direct the best of your energy there.

Conflict diminishes with clarity. We often see women struggle when one or two of their values compete with each other. When you are clear on what you value most, you are able to make better choices and understand the trade-offs. To do this, you must know what those values are and what you are willing to do to honor them. Security, making money, spirituality, recognition, altruism, power are all examples of values that are constantly in motion and at the root of the balance dilemma. That's why choices matter. Clarity matters.

One woman we coached knew she needed to take on a larger assignment in order to achieve her goal in the organization. She also was a mother of two and helped care for her mother-in-law under the same roof. She had a conflict between two equally significant values. She had to decide how to make it work.

MAKE COMMITMENTS CAREFULLY
Examine What You Say Yes To

Most women we coach don't have a time management problem; they have an overcommitment problem. Saying yes usually comes from a good place. We want to be helpful. We want to be good team players. We want to be the best. Saying no might disappoint someone in authority or a person you care about. But saying yes too often is neither healthy nor sustainable. Your energy can get sapped and your focus will begin to blur. Burnout becomes a big risk. Audit your calendar—and be brutal! For each event or meeting in your planner, ask: "Does this fit my values? Will it move me toward my goal? Does it have to be done by *me*?" If it doesn't, find a way to remove it or delegate. Consider that someone else might benefit from the experience. One woman Kathryn worked with spent precious time organizing a monthly team meeting long past the time when a younger associate could have, and arguably should have, taken over and benefited from the exposure. If the task must be done by you, does it have to be done soon or can it be delayed? Brenda coached a woman who did this exercise and realized she needed to delay her promotion for a year because she was caring for an elderly parent. Her values told her that a shift in focus and energy to her parent would make it harder to achieve success at work without exhausting herself. She negotiated a new start date for the promotion to go into effect.

Practice Saying No

This is the corollary to too many yes answers. Keep in mind that how you say no matters. If you can, offer a solution that aligns your goals with those of the person asking something from you. "John, I know it is important to you that we meet the financials we set for the year and I really need to focus on achieving my team's goals, too. I am unable to give that 100 percent right now, but I know someone who might help you if you're interested," or "I know you care about this and it is important to your goal, so I'd be happy to talk with Ed to try and line up resources for you."

Negotiate the Response Time

The dilemma about whether to say yes gets intensified when you feel pressured to give a quick turnaround, especially if you aren't clear about how the commitment will place added stress in your life. One woman Brenda coached confessed to having an immediate-turnaround habit. She considered it to be part of her reputationality. Every time her director asked for something, she leapt up and went to work. In one instance, she worked on a document until after midnight. After she delivered it, her supervisor responded, "Thank you, wonderful work as usual." When she replied, "I only wish I could've gotten this to you sooner," she was surprised when he answered, "No problem. I actually didn't need it until next week." That incident helped her see that everything doesn't have to be a fire drill. Instead of reacting immediately, she began to negotiate specific delivery times that she could reasonably build into her schedule.

REFRAME YOUR EXPECTATIONS

One woman Brenda worked with traveled extensively, as did her husband. They had two children, and when they were able to be all together, they wanted dinners to be special family times. Life's realities often interfered—a soccer game after work or the kids' after-school commitments at different locations—and she became frustrated. She felt like she wasn't the mother she wanted to be and started doubting her ability to handle it all. Then she had a thought. When she was growing up, her family had used the evening meal as a time to connect and converse. But why did that family time have to happen during the evening meal? When she realized that everyone tended to be together in the morning, the family decided to make breakfast their special family time. They began a tradition of having pancakes and eggs before everyone went on their way for the day. If something isn't working one way, try looking for unconventional ways to get what you need or want.

CREATE CRITERIA FOR MAKING DECISIONS

Think about your goals and values when you do this. We had a client who was inundated with invitations to work events every week. She felt overwhelmed by the ones she agreed to attend and guilty about the ones she couldn't go to. With coaching, she decided to institute a rule of committing to one evening event and one morning event per week. She carefully evaluated the events to see which most aligned with her values and priorities and politely declined the rest.

NEGOTIATE FOR FLEXIBILITY

This is big. In almost every organization and group of women we've coached, we've observed that the ability for women to negotiate for flexibility about important things can make a big difference. Some women have negotiated leaving the office at a certain time to pick up kids from school, then getting back online in the evening. Others have needed more options for travel schedules. If you are considering a role within a new organization, ask about flexibility. When you have identified what's important to you, you can often find ways to negotiate a winning outcome for all.

ASK FOR RESOURCES

We find that women—and this is backed by research—don't ask for what they need often enough and when they do, they don't ask big enough.[1] We offer this strategy to women we coach: describe what you want, offer solutions, stand your ground, and end with agreement. Often the request centers on more resources, more staff, additional budget, or a flexible schedule. Maybe you need a conversation, or sometimes a few, about what is on your plate and what needs to come off to make your life manageable. Often after our clients have these conversations, they report back to us that their boss has said, "Of course."

PRIORITIZE SELF-CARE

How do you feel when you are thriving? What does it look like when you are just surviving? No one is on either end of the spectrum 100 percent of the time, but you can consistently aim for the thriving end. Make a list of what helps you feel healthy and sane and what conditions are needed for you to be at your best. Then make a list of things that drain your energy and compare them. Choose wisely. Studies show that in the long run, the most productive people are those who take breaks and unplug from time to time.

GATHER YOUR POSSE

If you don't have the right support structure for where you are in life right now, consider who you can turn to—and who you might need to add to your posse—to create more work-life balance. Brenda's posse has a code for needing immediate help with career-related decisions called the "career 911." If her posse gets this text message, the phones start ringing. This is where ideas are exchanged, creative solutions get thrown around, and help kicks in.

There's truth-telling that goes on within a posse, in addition to commiseration, empathy, and the ability to add and share resources as needed.

Everything gets out of balance at times. In fact, the idea of balance is an illusion. It is more about flow and synchronicity of a full life. If you have done the work to assess and prioritize your values and create a support structure, you'll have a good sense of how to swing back to a manageable cadence when you need to. It requires intention. It requires you to align your values and your goals. It requires practice. But with consistent practice, you will see and feel a difference.

Light Your Own Broom

I raise up my voice—not so that I can shout, but so that those without a voice can be heard. We cannot all succeed when half of us are held back.

—MALALA YOUSAFZAI, NOBEL PRIZE LAUREATE AND ACTIVIST

Here is something we know: the world will be a better place with more women leaders.

The benefits and rewards of more women in leadership have been extensively researched and documented. The business case for this has been strongly asserted throughout this book. Effective women leaders inspire innovation, sustain profitability, manage risk, and create environments for inclusion and diversity to increase. These women leaders have learned how to thrive, and their presence in senior leadership helps to make businesses stronger.

For our women readers, our fervent wish is that YOU will become and remain one of them. We sincerely believe that the strategies we've outlined in this book will hasten your progress and your ascension into leadership. We've seen it happen for the thousands of clients we have coached. We feel confident it can happen for you.

We long for the day that books like this will be obsolete because effective women leaders have populated the corporate world. While we recognize that the world is constantly changing in ways that affect the way we work—the pandemic was a clear example of that—that only fuels our fire. We've never felt more committed and more urgent in our desire to help women succeed.

Research and statistics make it clear we still have a long way to go, and we know that women can't do it alone. *We want to emphatically acknowledge that the responsibility for making positive changes in the corporate world should not fall only on the shoulders of women.* Everyone has more work to do to raise awareness and invest energy in shifting company cultures and policies, regardless of their gender. We need systems to change. That's why we wrote this book.

Becoming a better leader means working on skills, searching for opportunities, and using your strengths. Imagine yourself with a clear perspective, a vision, and a strong sense of your story. What is the highest value you can bring? We encourage you to take a disciplined approach to preparing yourself, practicing, and performing with ease. Your confidence and ability to influence others can make a difference. And along the way, we encourage you to give back generously.

We've seen the good things that can happen when women do this. One example we love to talk about is a woman we'll call Dahlia, whom we've worked with for years. When we met, she was a senior leader with a bold and audacious goal. During a workshop we conducted, Dahlia confidently shared that she wanted to become CEO of her company. The women in the room laughed nervously. Had she really said that out loud? We looked at the others' faces, which seemed to say, "CEO! What is she thinking?" Today, she reports directly to the CEO, and she has altered her vision. Dahlia now wants to be chair of the board of directors because "it's a better job." She's never stopped working toward her goals even as she and her husband have juggled work and home duties while raising children.

Dahlia has called the strategies outlined in this book the "magic" that helped accelerate her career. She started with a vision. She is always on the lookout for ways to increase her self-awareness. Even today, she doggedly pursues proactive feedback, including consistently doing her own 360-degree assessments. She has established her reputationality and has created relevant messages about her achievements. When appropriate opportunities arise, she talks about them. She is meticulous about preparation and practice. She has surrounded herself with a posse she can turn to when she needs thought partners, advisors, or sympathetic ears. This is what it means to be deliberate.

A deliberate career starts with a clear sightline of where you'd like to end up. But remember, this is never cast in stone: changes can and will and should happen. Still, starting with a clear vision is crucial. Developing self-awareness and actively soliciting feedback to help you correct your course will be invaluable. Knowing what you want to be famous for, doing what's required to achieve that, and then broadcasting the information about who you are and where you want to go will alert the people who can help you. Find your people and use them. We call this a posse and you can call it whatever you want, but make sure you have people with diverse backgrounds and perspectives who are clear-eyed, supportive, and willing to give you honest feedback.

How you mix all of these strategies together is similar to making a stew. Although you add individual ingredients to the stew, it is the combination of spices and the process of simmering that makes it amazing. How you season the stew and stir the pot matters.

Start here and now. Focus on where you are and what you can do right now *for you*. Imagine what might be possible if you consistently tackled one or more of these strategies and did them well. Where could you be? What impact might you have? How many might hear your voice? Start with one practice, get good at it, then move to another. We've given you an abundance of strategies and we'll repeat our earlier caution: don't let yourself feel overwhelmed. We know you have plenty on your plate. Just choosing one or two things to work on with dedicated focus and practice will make a big difference. Even small changes will give you added lift and success.

Now you know this. You can do this. Remember, you don't have to tackle everything at once. Look for the blind spots that have become impediments to your deliberate career. Make one or two strategies a part of your routine. Practice, then practice some more. As is the case when learning any skill, once you develop muscle memory, it becomes part of you. When you've become adept, move on to the next. With patience and time and mastery of new skills, managing your career will seem less overwhelming. You will own your career and your outcomes with fresh energy.

We continue to keep the broom lit. We're out here waving it. We're rooting for you. We encourage you to light your own broom and extend a hand to other women along the way.

Go bold. Aim high. Be courageous. We can't wait to see the world you create.

I Wish I'd Known This

Discussion Guide

One thing we know about highly effective leaders is that they take time to reflect. We recommend this skill for anyone who wants to improve. Now that you have read through the blind spots, strategies, and coaching tips, here are questions for reflection for an individual leader and questions that can be used in group discussions. Such group conversations are learning zones for all of us; they give us space to share experiences, leverage the knowledge of others, and integrate the best of everything.

INDIVIDUAL DISCUSSION GUIDE

What drew you to this book?

Rate yourself on the areas in the questions below and reflect on why you rated yourself that way.

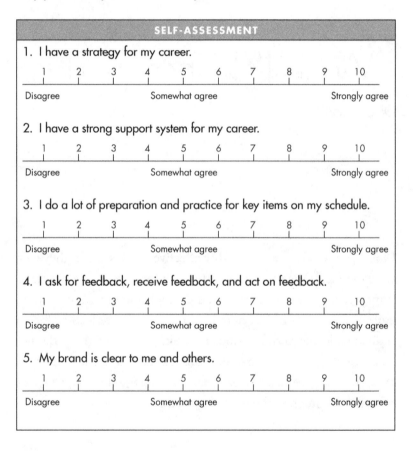

Which of the stories in the book most resonated with you and why?

Which strategies do you feel most confident about?

Which strategies do you feel least confident about?

Which strategy do you think would give you the most "lift"?

What are your internal voices telling you and how do they influence your actions or decisions?

Can you identify stories you are telling yourself or limiting beliefs that contribute to the blind spots?

What strategies or coaching tips will you incorporate in your career?

Now that you're aware of the blind spots, what do you need to change about your stories so you can move forward?

Who do you tend to go to for career support and advice? How could you expand this list?

What three actions could you take that would have the biggest long-term impact on your career?

What do you need to add to your career toolbox in order to be successful? What might you need to let go of?

GROUP DISCUSSION GUIDE

What in the book sounded or felt familiar about how women lead and work in your environment?

What do you see in the workplace that could be possible stumbling blocks for women leaders who seek to maximize their influence?

Discuss some of the ways you have seen women's achievements being undervalued and what might be changed to highlight their contributions.

How can women in the workplace support each other? What actions could be taken to move the number higher on the scale?

Share which story in the book resonated with you the most and why.

Share with each other which of the blind spots you need to work on most and what strategies you will use to address them.

As you share your internal stories, what commonalities and differences do you see among the group?

Talk about the methods that women use to amplify their messages that were described in the book. Which ones resonated with your experience?

In what other ways might you help and support the women you work with to build leadership capacity in yourself and others?

Discuss the ways people have positively influenced your career or ways you have influenced someone else in their career. What specific actions were effective?

Which of the suggestions in the book can you take today that would contribute positively to a successful, sustainable career?

Notes

Introduction

1. McKinsey & Company and LeanIn.Org, *Women in the Workplace: 2021* (N.p.: McKinsey and Company, 2021).

2. McKinsey and Company and LeanIn.Org, *Women in the Workplace: 2021*, 7, 12, 38, 50.

3. McKinsey and Company and LeanIn.Org, *Women in the Workplace: 2021*, 7.

4. McKinsey and Company and LeanIn.Org, *Women in the Workplace: 2021*, 7.

5. Mary Davis Holt, Jill Flynn, and Kathryn Heath, *Break Your Own Rules: How to Change the Patterns of Thinking That Block Women's Paths to Power* (San Francisco: Jossey-Bass, 2011), 2–3.

6. Roy Adler, "Women in the Executive Suite Correlate to High Profits," *Harvard Business Review* 79, no. 3 (2001): 30–32.

7. Cristian L. Dezső and David Gaddis Ross, "Does Female Representation in Top Management Improve Firm Performance? A Panel Data Investigation," *Strategic Management Journal* 33, no. 9 (2012): 1072–1089.

8. Sundiatu Dixon-Fyle, Kevin Dolan, Vivian Hunt, and Sara Prince, "Diversity Wins: How Inclusion Matters," McKinsey & Company, May 19, 2020, https://www.mckinsey.com/featured-insights/ diversity-and-inclusion/diversity-wins-how-inclusion-matters.

9. Natacha Catalino and Kirstan Marnane, "When Women Lead, Workplaces Should Listen," McKinsey & Company, December 11, 2019, https://www.mckinsey.com/featured-insights/leadership/ when-women-lead-workplaces-should-listen.

10. *Groundhog Day,* directed by Harold Ramis (Hollywood, CA: Columbia Studios, 1993).

11. Malcolm Gladwell, *Outliers: The Story of Success* (New York: Little, Brown & Co., 2008), 35–68.

12. Nicholas Salter, "A Brief History of Female Fortune 500 CEOs," Lead Read Today, Fisher College of Business, Ohio State University, https://fisher.osu.edu/blogs/leadreadtoday/a-brief-history-female -fortune-500-ceos; Nina Stoller-Lindsey, "Trailblazing Women Who Broke the Glass Ceiling in the Business and Finance Sectors," *Forbes Magazine,* March 7, 2017.

13. Catalyst, "Historical List of Women CEOs of the Fortune Lists: 1972–2021," June 2021, https://www.catalyst.org/research/ historical-list-of-women-ceos-of-the-fortune-lists-1972-2021/.

14. Holt, Flynn, and Heath, *Break Your Own Rules.*

15. Roy D'Adler, "Women in the Executive Suite Correlate to High Profits," *Harvard Business Review* 79, no. 3 (2001): 30–32; Lois Joy, Nancy M. Carter, Harvey M. Wagner, and Sriram Wagner, *The Bottom Line: Corporate Performance and Women's Representation on Boards*, Catalyst report, October 2007: https://www.catalyst.org/ research/the-bottom-line-corporate-performance-and-womens -representation-on-boards/; Cristian L. Dezső and David Gaddis Ross, "Does Female Representation in Top Management Improve Firm Performance? A Panel Data Investigation?," unpublished article, https://www0.gsb.columbia.edu/mygsb/faculty/research/ pubfiles/3063/female_representation.pdf.

16. McKinsey and Company and LeanIn.Org, *Women in the Workplace: 2021*, 8.

Chapter 1

1. Wei Zheng, Ronit Kark, and Alyson Meister, "How Women Manage the Gendered Norms of Leadership," *Harvard Business Review*, November 28, 2018, https://hbr.org/2018/11/how-women-manage-the-gendered-norms-of-leadership.

2. Dasie J. Schultz and Christine Enslin, "The Female Executive's Perspective on Career Planning and Advancement in Organizations: Experiences with Cascading Gender Bias, the Double-Bind, and Unwritten Rules to Advancement," *SAGE Open* 4, no. 4 (2014), https://journals.sagepub.com/doi/full/10.1177/2158244014558040.

3. Conversation with Lynne Ford.

4. Michael Lombardo and Robert Eichinger, *The Leadership Machine* (Minneapolis: Lominger, 2005).

5. Marshall Goldsmith, *What Got You Here Won't Get You There* (New York: Hachette Books, 2007).

6. Ursula Burns, *Where You Are Is Not Who You Are* (New York: Amistad Publishing, 2021).

7. Herminia Ibarra and Otilia Obodaru, "Women and the Vision Thing," *Harvard Business Review* (January 2009), https://hbr.org/2009/01/women-and-the-vision-thing.

Chapter 2

1. Tasha Eurich, "What Self-Awareness Really Is (And How to Cultivate It)," *Harvard Business Review*, January 4, 2018, https://hbr.org/2018/01/what-self-awareness-really-is-and-how-to-cultivate-it.

2. Eurich, "What Self-Awareness Really Is."

3. Eurich, "What Self-Awareness Really Is."

4. Brené Brown, *The Gifts of Imperfection: Let Go of Who You Think You're Supposed to Be and Embrace Who You Are* (Minneapolis: Hazelden Publishing, 2010). Quote from Brené Brown, *Daring Greatly: How the Courage to Be Vulnerable Transforms the Way We Live, Love, Parent, and Lead* (New York: Avery, 2012), 294.

5. Robert W. Eichinger and Michael M. Lombardo, *The Career Architect Development Planner*, 5th ed. (Dallas: Lominger International, 2010), 857.

6. Shanna Hocking, "Why Women Need to Ask for Better Feedback, More Often," *Harvard Business Review*, September 10, 2021, https://hbr.org/2021/09/why-women-need-to-ask-for-better -feedback-more-often.

7. Tasha Eurich, "Why Self-Awareness Isn't Doing More to Help Women's Careers," *Harvard Business Review*, May 31, 2019, https:// hbr.org/2019/05/why-self-awareness-isnt-doing-more-to-help -womens-careers.

8. Joseph Folkman, "Top Ranked Leaders Know This Secret: Ask For Feedback," *Forbes*, January 8, 2015, https://www.forbes.com/sites/ joefolkman/2015/01/08/top-ranked-leaders-know-this-secret-ask -for-feedback/?sh=238e27873195.

9. Mary Davis Holt, Jill Flynn, and Kathryn Heath, *Break Your Own Rules: How to Change the Patterns of Thinking That Block Women's Paths to Power* (San Francisco: Jossey-Bass, 2011).

10. Kirsten Weir, "Give Me a Break: Psychologists Explore the Type and Frequency of Breaks We Need to Refuel Our Energy and Enhance Our Well-Being," *Monitor on Psychology* 50, no. 1 (2019), https://www.apa.org/monitor/2019/01/break.

11. "The Double-Bind Dilemma for Women in Leadership (Infographic)," Catalyst: Workplaces that Work for Women," August 2, 2018, https://www.catalyst.org/research/infographic-the -double-bind-dilemma-for-women-in-leadership/.

12. Pat Olsen, "How to Overcome the 'Double Bind,'" Diversity Women Media, February 21, [2021], https://www.diversitywoman .com/how-to-overcome-the-double-blind/.

13. Jane Edison Stevenson and Evelyn Orr, "We Interviewed 57 Female CEOs to Find Out How More Women Can Get to the Top," *Harvard Business Review*, November 8, 2017.

14. Maren Showkeir and Jamie Showkeir, *Yoga Wisdom at Work: Finding Sanity Off the Mat and On the Job* (Oakland, CA: Berrett-Koehler, 2013), 136.

15. Stephen R. Covey, *The Seven Habits of Highly Effective People*, 4th ed. (New York: Simon & Schuster, 2020).

Chapter 3

1. Steuart Henderson Britt and Harper W. Boyd Jr., *Marketing Management and Administrative Action* (New York: McGraw-Hill, 1973).

2. Stéphanie Thomson, "A Lack of Confidence Isn't What's Holding Back Working Women," *Atlantic*, September 20, 2018, https://www .theatlantic.com/family/archive/2018/09/women-workplace -confidence-gap/570772/.

3. Meghan I. H. Lindeman, Amanda M. Durik, and Maura Dooley, "Women and Self-Promotion: A Test of Three Theories," *Psychological Reports* 122, no. 1 (2019): 219–230, https://journals. sagepub.com/doi/pdf/10.1177/0033294118755096.

4. David McNally and Karl Speak, *Be Your Own Brand* (Oakland, CA: Berrett-Koehler, 2001), 4.

5. Lida Citroën, *Control the Narrative: The Executive's Guide to Building, Pivoting and Repairing Your Reputation* (London: Kogan Page, 2021), 1.

6. PR Newswire, "More Than Half of Employers Have Found Content on Social Media That Caused Them NOT to Hire a Candidate, According to Recent CareerBuilder Survey," press release, CareerBuilder.com, August 9, 2018, https://press.careerbuilder. com/2018-08-09-More-Than-Half-of-Employers-Have-Found- Content-on-Social-Media-That-Caused-Them-NOT-to-Hire-a- Candidate-According-to-Recent-CareerBuilder-Survey.

Chapter 4

1. Elena Doldor, Madeleine Wyatt, and Jo Silvester, "Research: Men Get More Actionable Feedback Than Women," *Harvard Business Review*, February 10, 2021, https://hbr.org/2021/02/ research-men-get-more-actionable-feedback-than-women.

2. Doldor, Wyatt, and Silvester, "Research: Men Get More Actionable Feedback Than Women."

3. Sylvia Boorstein, "What We Nurture," On Being, May 5, 2011, updated May 9, 2019, https://onbeing.org/programs/sylvia-boorstein-what-we-nurture/.

4. Boorstein, "What We Nurture."

5. Robert W. Eichinger and Michael M. Lombardo, *The Career Architect Development Planner*, 5th ed. (Dallas: Lominger International, 2010).

6. David A. Garvin, "The U.S. Army's After Action Reviews: Seizing the Chance to Learn," excerpt from Garvin, *Learning in Action, A Guide to Putting the Learning Organization to Work* (Boston: Harvard Business School Press, 2000), 106–116, https://www.nwcg.gov/sites/default/files/wfldp/docs/army-seizing-chance-to-learn.pdf.

Chapter 5

1. Alexandra Carter and Janet O'Shea, eds., *The Routledge Dance Studies Reader*, 2nd ed. (Routledge, 2010), 96.

2. Kathryn Heath, Jill Flynn, and Mary Davis Holt, "Women, Find Your Voice," *Harvard Business Review* (June 2014), https://hbr.org/2014/06/women-find-your-voice.

3. Tim S. Grover, *Relentless: From Good to Great to Unstoppable* (New York: Scribner, 2014).

4. Kathryn Heath, Jill Flynn, Mary David Holt, and Diana Faison, *The Influence Effect: A New Path to Power for Women Leaders* (Oakland, CA: Berrett-Koehler, 2017).

5. Angie Flynn-McIver, *Before You Say Anything: How to Have Better Conversations, Love Public Speaking, and Finally Know What to Do with Your Hands* ([Asheville, NC]: Nutgraf Productions, 2021).

Chapter 6

1. Yang Yang, Nitesh V. Chawla, and Brian Uzzi, "A Network's Gender Composition and Communication Pattern Predict Women's Leadership Success," *PNAS: Proceedings of the National Academy of Sciences of the United States of America* 116, no. 6 (2019), https://www.pnas.org/content/116/6/2033.

2. Kristen Hicks, "Why Professional Networking Groups for Women Remain Valuable," *Fast Company*, January 7, 2020, https://www.fastcompany.com/90448654/the-benefits-of-womens-networking-groups.

3. Robert W. Eichinger and Michael M. Lombardo, *The Career Architect Development Planner*, 5th ed. (Dallas: Lominger International, 2010).

4. See Alexandra Michel, "Burnout and the Brain," Association for Psychological Science, January 29, 2016, https://www.psychologicalscience.org/observer/burnout-and-the-brain.

5. Glenda Mcdonald, Debra Jackson, Margaret H. Vickers, and Lesley Wilkes, "Surviving Workplace Adversity: A Qualitative Study of Nurses and Midwives and Their Strategies to Increase Personal Resilience," *Journal of Nursing Management*, April 13, 2015, https://onlinelibrary.wiley.com/doi/abs/10.1111/jonm.12293. See also "How Burnout Affects Women," The WellRight Blog, November 20, 2019, https://www.wellright.com/blog/how-burnout-affects-women. See also Corporate Counsel Women of Color, "Overworked and Stressed 5 Strategies to Manage Burnout," April 6, 2021, https://ccwomenofcolor.org/fitness/overworked-and-stressed-5-strategies-to-manage-burnout/.

6. David Rock and Heidi Grant, "Why Diverse Teams Are Smarter," *Harvard Business Review*, November 4, 2016, https://hbr.org/2016/11/why-diverse-teams-are-smarter.

7. Herminia Ibarra, "A Lack of Sponsorship Is Keeping Women from Advancing into Leadership," *Harvard Business Review*, August 19, 2019, https://hbr.org/2019/08/a-lack-of-sponsorship-is-keeping-women-from-advancing-into-leadership.

8. Ibarra, "A Lack of Sponsorship Is Keeping Women from Advancing into Leadership."

9. Juliet Eilperin, "White House Women Want to Be in the Room Where It Happens," *Washington Post*, September 13, 2016, https://www.washingtonpost.com/news/powerpost/wp/2016/09/13/white-house-women-are-now-in-the-room-where-it-happens/.

Chapter 7

1. Linda Babcock and Sara Laschever, *Women Don't Ask: Negotiation and the Gender Divide* (Princeton, NJ: Princeton University Press, 2021).

Acknowledgments

The first of many thanks goes out to you, the reader. You accompanied us on this journey, and our primary wish is that the ideas in this book will travel with you, advancing you and the women you support, sponsor, coach, and work beside every day. We want you to be successful, to have maximum impact in all you do, and maybe even light a torch for those behind you.

We appreciate and admire each of the thousands of women we have had the privilege to coach. They have worked tirelessly to have a profound impact on their respective worlds and have shared their experiences courageously. We thank the organizations we've worked with that have stayed the course in supporting women and advancing female talent. They are making strategic investments in the future. The work goes on.

We thank our friend and colleague, Bravanti President and CEO Susan Gallagher and the entire Bravanti team for being supporters, sponsors, and champions of moving women forward faster. Without them, this work might not have come to fruition. We work to ignite bold futures, and never has there been a more inspiring mission in our history.

A special thanks to Anna Leinberger for encouraging us to pursue this book. She asked hard questions and made us and this book better. Also, our appreciation to Neal Maillet, our editor at Berrett-Koehler for pulling us through to the end. Their guidance and support pushed us to capture universal themes and serve them back up to women of all levels, geographies, industries, and backgrounds.

Our deepest gratitude to our collaborator, Maren Showkeir, for finding our voices, helping us stay the course, and taking us across the finish line. Her humor, wisdom, and candor were a regular tonic. We can't imagine where we would be without her.

Kate Babbitt made us better line by line, point by point. She is amazingly talented and we have been fortunate to work with her.

Many thanks to Becky Robinson of Weaving Influence for working to get this book into many hands. Deep appreciation to Jill Flynn, Diana Faison, Tina Powell, Kasey Stewart, Kati Hollifield, Ann Morris, and all our consultants who facilitate our work with women. They have created and perpetuated a legacy of women helping women—and it is powerful.

How can we ever find the words to acknowledge our spouses, families, friends, and colleagues? You have supported, critiqued, challenged, and embraced the work with us. Our hearts swell with gratitude for your encouragement and for the sacrifices you made as we devoted time to this work. The depth of our respect, love, and appreciation is endless.

Finally, our deepest admiration goes out to every generation of women in the workforce, to women from every walk of life, and to every woman who has ever been an "only" in a room of many. May we all find our voice and use it fulfill our own aspirations and to create a better, brighter future for all those beside and behind us.

Index

About the Authors

Brenda Wensil is a recognized expert on women's leadership and dedicated to advancing women in the workforce. She is a managing director and heads the Leadership Acceleration practice at Bravanti, a preeminent firm in the field of leadership development.

Wensil served in numerous executive leadership roles in the financial services industry, including head of Customer Strategy for Wachovia, creating successful customer growth and retention strategies, developing brand, and expanding retail banking into new markets. She also developed and led global supply chain management programs for Barclays Bank in London. Wensil was the first-named chief customer experience officer at the U.S. Department of Education,

Office of Federal Student Aid in Washington D.C. She received the 2012 Executive Leadership Award from the U.S. secretary of education and was awarded the Service to the Citizen Award for customer experience in the federal arena.

Wensil has authored numerous articles on women's leadership and inclusive leadership behaviors for *Harvard Business Review*. She is a frequent keynote speaker and panelist on the topic of women's leadership and customer experience strategy.

Wensil holds a master's degree in organization development and executive coaching from the McColl School of Business at Queens University of Charlotte and a BA in journalism from the University of South Carolina. She is a Professional Certified Coach by the International Coaching Federation and a Board Certified Coach by the Center for Credentialing and Education. She is a senior fellow of the American Leadership Forum and a graduate of the Executive Leadership Program at the Kenan-Flagler Business School, University of North Carolina at Chapel Hill.

Kathryn Heath, PhD, is a distinguished thought leader, author, and sought-after speaker on the topic of women's leadership. For more than twenty years, she has coached high-potential women leaders to help them move forward faster. She is a coauthor of *The Influence Effect: A New Path to Power for Women Leaders* (Berrett-Koehler, 2017) and *Break Your Own Rules: How to Change the Patterns of Thinking That Block Women's Path to Power* (Jossey-Bass, 2011). She also authored five chapters in the *HBR Guide for Women at Work* (Harvard Business Review Press, 2019).

Heath currently serves as a managing director of the Leadership Acceleration Practice at Bravanti. She was a founding partner of Flynn Heath Leadership, where she designed and executed custom programs to recruit, retain, and promote women and to help women overcome barriers to advancement. Previously, Heath was senior vice-president and director of First University at First Union, where her inventive and results-focused approach won her numerous awards in the field of learning and development.

Heath has also coauthored numerous articles on women's leadership for *Harvard Business Review.* She is a high-demand speaker for conference keynotes and other events, and she has presented at the 24th Annual ICAN Women's Leadership Conference and the Network of Executive Women Leadership Summit.

Heath holds a PhD from the University of North Carolina Greensboro; a master's degree in education from the University of North Carolina at Charlotte; and a BA from the University of North Carolina at Chapel Hill.

About Bravanti

The authors of *I Wish I'd Known This* are both managing directors at Bravanti, a global leadership development and executive coaching organization. Bravanti was founded almost forty years ago to support leaders in their quest to have more impact. We help leaders, teams, and organizations find the power within to lead bravely, be prepared to meet challenges, and seize opportunities in a continually uncertain business environment.

Bravanti has a specialized team dedicated to the unique challenges women and other historically underrepresented groups face in their leadership journeys. This team of former high-powered women executives (including the authors of this book) designs customized leadership acceleration and coaching programs to help organizations retain, develop, and advance women and underrepresented groups into leadership roles.

Thought leaders on this team have published two previous books on women's leadership: *Break Your Own Rules: How to*

Change the Patterns of Thinking That Block Women's Paths to Power, and *The Influence Effect: A New Path to Power for Women Leaders.* Other thought leadership includes several chapters in the *HBR Guide for Women at Work* and more than ten articles in *Harvard Business Review.*

Bravanti is a preeminent provider of an array of executive coaching, leadership acceleration, and career coaching services. The firm is headquartered in Chicago with 1,000 consultants in thirty countries around the world. Learn more at www.bravanti.com.

Dear reader,

Thank you for picking up this book and welcome to the worldwide BK community! You're joining a special group of people who have come together to create positive change in their lives, organizations, and communities.

What's BK all about?

Our mission is to connect people and ideas to create a world that works for all.

Why? Our communities, organizations, and lives get bogged down by old paradigms of self-interest, exclusion, hierarchy, and privilege. But we believe that can change. That's why we seek the leading experts on these challenges—and share their actionable ideas with you.

A welcome gift

To help you get started, we'd like to offer you a **free copy** of one of our bestselling ebooks:

www.bkconnection.com/welcome

When you claim your **free ebook**, you'll also be subscribed to our blog.

Our freshest insights

Access the best new tools and ideas for leaders at all levels on our blog at ideas.bkconnection.com.

Sincerely,

Your friends at Berrett-Koehler

Certified

Corporation